LA GRANGE

John D Troyer
5-24-96

See chapters 8 and 9 for more information about the Perkins' family and the bank.

A PICTORIAL HISTORY OF
LaGRANGE COUNTY, INDIANA

By Sandy Yoder
Robert Yoder, photographer

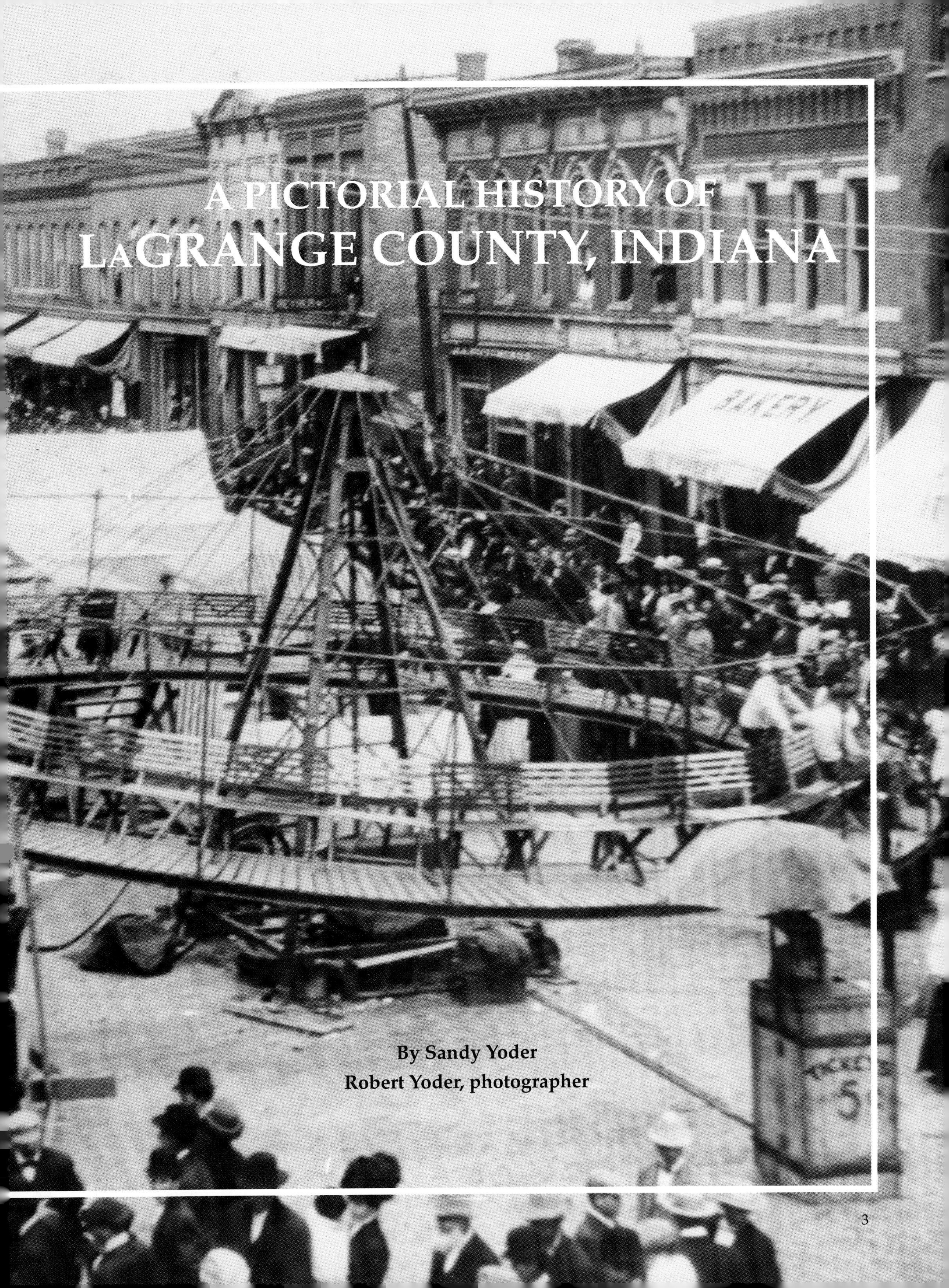

Endsheet photo
These LaGrange High School boys, complete with bat boy, won the Northeastern Indiana Athletic Association title in 1910. Members of the LaGrange team were: Ernest Holland, first base; Demorest Ruick, second base; Gage, shortstop; Somerlott, third base; Smith, left field; Schermerhorn, center field; Shirley, right field; Davidson, pitcher; Ray Fisher, catcher (back row, third from right); Sams, substitute; and E. R. Somerlott, coach. Gifford Photo; courtesy of Rex Fisher.

Title page photo
The school children paraded on Detroit Street at Corn School in 1911. Christian Giggy is the man with the white beard (bottom, right of center) behind the lady with the large black hat. Gifford photo; courtesy of Rex Fisher.

For information write:

The Donning Company/Publishers
184 Business Park Drive, Suite 106
Virginia Beach, Virginia 23462

Steve Mull, General Manager
Bob Jonson, Project Director
Laura Hill, Research Consultant
Mair Downing, Project Research Coordinator
Mary Jo Kurten, Editor
Mary Elizabeth Apperson, Art Director
Dawn V. Kofroth, Production Manager
Tony Lillis, Director of Marketing

Library of Congress Cataloging-in-Publication Data

Yoder, Sandra, 1944–
A pictorial history of LaGrange County, Indiana / by Sandra Yoder.
p. cm.
Includes bibliographical references (p.) and index.
ISBN 0-89865-958-2 (alk. paper)
1. LaGrange County (Ind.)—History—Pictorial works. 2. LaGrange County (Ind.)—History I. Title.
F532.L17Y63 1996
977.2'79—dc20
96-44051
CIP

Printed in the United States of America

Table of Contents

Willis Sams and his threshing rig are at the Pius Long farm in 1912. It is the present home of Mr. and Mrs. Gordon Olds of 1645E 150N in Bloomfield Township. At left is Io Long and her little daughter, Madola (Long) Sprague. Pius Long is the first man left of center with the dog nearby. Gifford photo; courtesy of Irene (Nelson) Babcock.

Preface

LaGrange County is built on a strong foundation of adventuresome people. This book is a glimpse of some of the men and women who have shaped our county's development. The photographs we received show hard workers: farmers, soldiers, founders of towns, animals, and children. It was difficult to choose among them—especially the hundreds received from Bloomfield Township alone.

We hope this book will encourage others to mark their family pictures and preserve the paper trail left by earlier residents. Future generations will appreciate the effort.

This home was given to the LaGrange County Historical Society as a bequest in Inez Machan's will upon her death in 1985. Her grandmother, Mary Devlin, purchased the land in 1875 from John Ryason, developer of Ryason's Additions to the town of LaGrange. Mrs. Devlin and husband James got the idea for this house at the U.S. Centennial Exposition in 1876. Located on South Poplar Street, the house has a modified Southern style. Mrs. Harold Machan acquired the home from her mother, Eva (Mrs. Frank Sitters). The Historical Society operates it as the Inez Machan Museum. Yoder photo.

Acknowledgments

The Donning Company/Publishers worked with the LaGrange County Historical Society, Inc., to secure a sponsor for this publication. The Farmers State Bank agreed that a pictorial history of our county would be a way to preserve the past and entertain the reader simultaneously. The bank generously offered to undertake the publishing costs with profits going to the Historical Society. Miles Perkins, bank president, along with his wife, Judy, loaned pictures for the publication and shared information with us. Members of the local Historical Society brought pictures from their personal collections. Among them were Richard and Lisa Tjarks, J. Scott McKibben, Norma Tressler, Irene Babcock, Lela Stanner, Dorothy Harris, Madola Sprague, Mary McCormick, Richard Kelly, and Russell Frehse.

Rex Fisher and Wilma Ellis donated pictures from Clay Township and other places. Rena Markley provided pictures from Newbury, Mrs. Robert Simpson had many pictures from her late husband's collection from Van Buren and Newbury Townships, and Blanche Myers had information and pictures from Van Buren Township. Marian Deal contributed Springfield pictures, among others. Janice Olinghouse Keller came all the way from Ohio to bring family pictures. Others were Kathryn Bloom, Katherine Swartzentruber, Clara Hirschy, Beverly Warner, Nina Eash, Margie and Gordon Frost, Roberta May, Denise McNabb, Glen Smith, and Carl Dintaman. Richard Marks sent pictures, several of which were from the Gerald Fisher collection. Ruth and Verne Schlemmer shared their albums and slides of LaGrange County. The LaGrange County Historical Society also contributed pictures.

Nancy Stump provided a copy of *The Stroh Times* (1901). The LaGrange postmaster, John Cochard, and maintenance personnel with ladders, enabled us to secure a photograph of the mural in the lobby. A special thanks goes to these men for their patience. Kenneth Workman, principal, and Deanna Johnson, guidance director, both from Prairie Heights High School, allowed me to work a flexible schedule so work on the book could proceed. Monty Glick made last minute enlargments and made these pictures look better than the originals. My husband, Robert, repeatedly complied with my requests to snap just one more picture. Of course, the staff of the Donning Company/Publishers provided guidelines and advice vital to the book's success. Thank you, thank you.

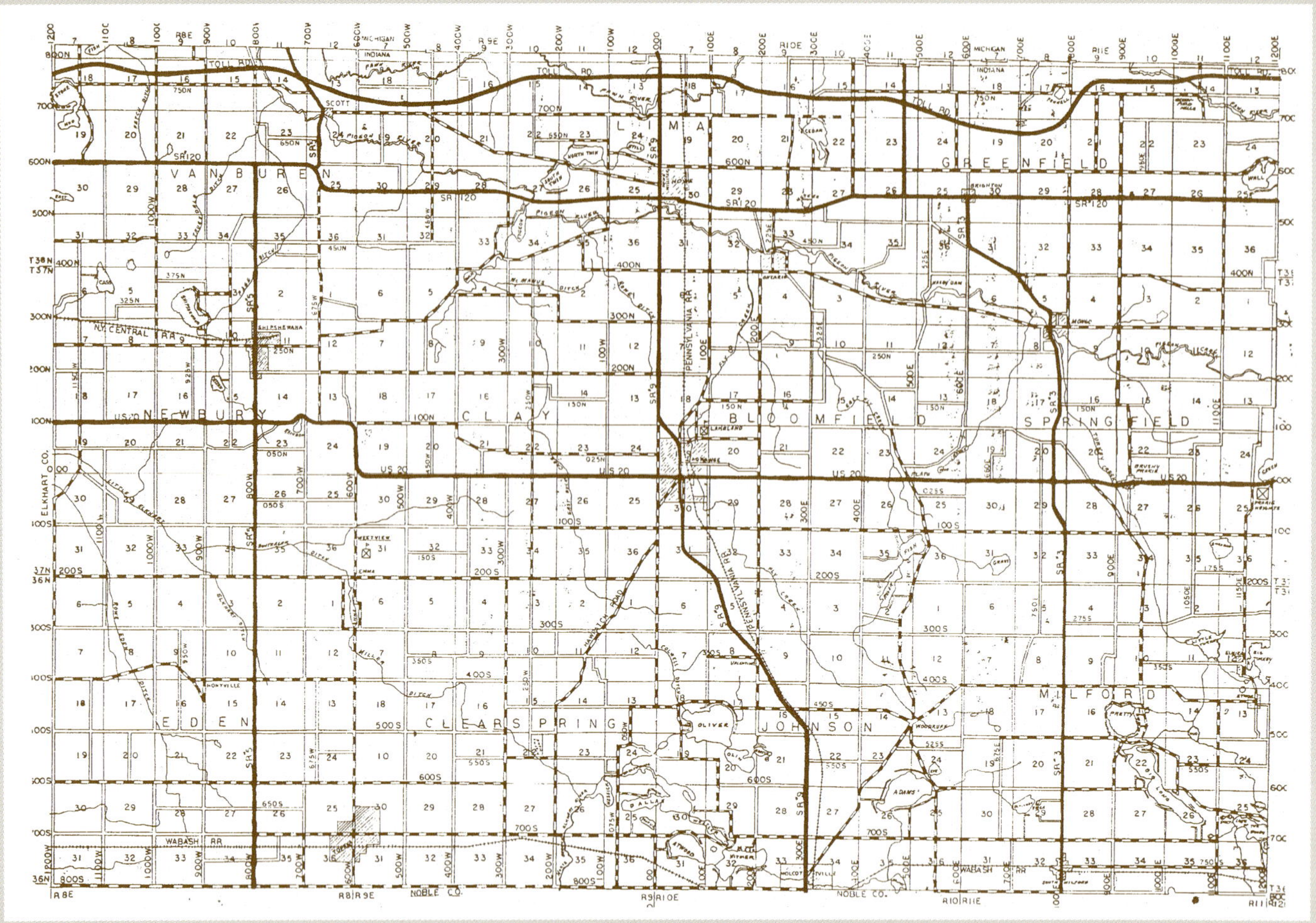

Edwin B. Houck, County Engineer and Surveyor, made this map of LaGrange County in 1970. Courtesy of Scott McKibben.

Introduction

LaGrange County is located in northeast Indiana halfway between Chicago and Detroit. The Indiana East-West Toll Road passes across the northern part of the county. U.S. 20 parallels it through the center, and State Road 9 cuts it in half from north to south. State Roads 5 and 3 also pass through the county. It is bordered on the north by Michigan, which once claimed a strip ten miles deep across the northern part. Farms, small industries, lakes, and woods cover the area. Pigeon River Fish and Game Preserve is a popular attraction for nature lovers to hunt, fish, hike, canoe, and watch wildlife.

The western part of the county is comprised mostly of Amish and Mennonites who follow a conservative lifestyle. The roads are traveled by a conglomeration of trucks, cars, and horses and buggies. The town of Shipshewana is one of the biggest tourist attractions in the state due to its livestock auction, flea market, and antique shops.

Many businesses are tied to the mobile home, travel home, and modular home industries or "trailer factories" as the locals call them. Farmland is more costly than it used to be so some people have left farming to work in factories. Some of the Amish people have moved to Wisconsin where land is more plentiful. Others have started woodworking shops or do carpentry work.

Public and private schools exist side by side. There are three public school corporations, one military school, and about thirty-four small Amish schools. College credit may be earned in the county through satellite schools, but no colleges are here at the present time.

If we travel into the past, however, we will see a flourishing college town, a home for communal living, woolen- and gristmills, lumberyards, huge forests, Indians, pioneers, log cabins, oxen, and wagons. Life revolved around churches, schools, families, and towns. Let's visit, through pictures, the world of our ancestors.

Joseph William Connelly (seated) came to LaGrange County with his parents, Rev. Thomas Birch Connelly and Savilla (Groves) Connelly and sisters Mary (later Parker) and Martha (later Jacobs). They arrived from Madison County, Ohio, on August 5, 1835, and settled in Bloomfield Township. Louisa (Gage) Connelly (seated) was born in LaGrange County to Jacob and Anna (Eastlick) Gage. Joseph and Louisa had ten children. (Mary Roxina died in infancy.) Standing left to right are Savilla McGinnis, Orphus J., Hiram J., Charles F., Martha Salina Skeer, Byron T., John B., Joseph Albert (Al), and Orpha M. Weir. Hiram and Byron were twins. So were Orpha and Orphus. Artists Co-operative Association photo; courtesy of the Connelly family.

1

Bloomfield Township

Potawatomi Indians lived in the area of Indiana now called LaGrange County long before white settlers came to claim the land. In the late 1820s and early 1830s, newcomers from the settled eastern states began to arrive. At first they coexisted with the Indians who hunted and fished on the lakes and along the rivers. For several years, the two peoples traded supplies and traveled the old buffalo trails together. Alcohol and disease, however, began to plague both races.

At first there was room for everyone to dwell and make a living. The forests were thick and the axes were ready to cut wood for building log homes and for clearing cropland. Conservation was unknown.

The settlers wanted to own the land and rule one another. In June 1835, Bloomfield was organized as a civil township. The first village to be platted was Burlington, a "paper town," platted by William C. Tillman in section 1 in May of 1836. It was advertised, according to the *History of Northeast Indiana, Vol. I,* as being "on Pigeon River, which was of sufficient size to utilize shipping by good sized boats." Town lots were sold, but no village ever materialized.

On June 18 of the same year, the town of LaGrange was platted in section 19 by Reuben J. Dawson, William F. Beavers, George F. Whittaker, and James McConnell. The land of the original platt first belonged to George F. Whittaker and Theodore Craft. Joshua T. Hobbs later bought an interest. Lots were sold and the town flourished.

The village of Bloomfield was platted in section 23 on September 14, also in the year 1836, by Moses J. Hill and Ivory Crandall. They thought the county seat might be located there. When this did not happen and the railroad bypassed the area, town lots were not developed. (Bloomfield village was in the same general area as the place that became known as "Hill's Corners" and later as Plato.) A cluster of families settled there, nonetheless. A sawmill, grocery store, cemetery, churches, and hall were eventually located nearby.

The Plato Store was a grocery owned by Bernard and Mariam Bassett during the 1950s and 1960s. Schlemmer photo; courtesy of Verne Schlemmer.

Plato Hall was used for community and church activities. On April 26, 1907, it held the third annual commencement of Bloomfield Township High School. The graduates were Bertha Garmire, Ralph Hilterbrant, May Stolebarger, Archie Jones, Laura Sears, W. Vern Elliott, George Anderson, Mary Weir, and Fred Hamilton. The hall was demolished circa 1986. Courtesy of Marian Deal.

Right
The building shown here is the third LaGrange County Courthouse. The first frame one was built in 1833, in Lima (Howe). When LaGrange became the county seat, a two-story frame building with cupola was completed in 1844. This current courthouse was ready for court on November 13, 1879, at a cost of $71,675.32. It is on the National Register of Historic Places. Photo circa 1915; courtesy of Margie Frost.

In 1838, according to *A Patchwork Sampler*, the United States government relocated the Potawatomis to Kansas near the Osage River. Thirty-eight Indians died on the way. For the survivors, a way of life was nearing extinction.

In the same year as the village plattings, 1836, the LaGrange Collegiate Institute was organized in Ontario by Nathan Jenks. It opened in 1839. Although Ontario is in Lima Township, the college was just over the township line in Bloomfield.

In LaGrange County, the town of LaGrange soon replaced Lima as county seat. A frame courthouse was built at LaGrange in 1843. The county offices moved there in 1844.

In the same year, Charles B. Holmes settled in LaGrange. He was the first postmaster, the first merchant, and the first justice of the peace in the new county seat. Lawyers, doctors, preachers, and other merchants followed him. The *LaGrange Standard*, a county newspaper, was established in 1857 by John K. Morrow to serve the needs of townspeople as well as the farming community. It still exists in 1995.

Bloomfield became the most populated township in the county. It was the site of the first enrollment of volunteers when the Civil War erupted. On April 20, 1861, Dr. J. H. Rerick drew up the first company roll at LaGrange. Eager to end the rebellion, county men quickly gathered to join the regiments. Space does not permit an exhaustive list, but the following regiments were heavily populated by LaGrange men: 21st (1st Heavy Artillery), 30th, 44th, 88th, 100th, 127th (12th Cavalry), 129th, and 152nd. In this war and the ones to follow, the deaths and injuries were hard to bear, but the battles were fought bravely and the soldiers deserving of glory.

Just prior to the Civil War, railroad promoters sold stock and planned routes through LaGrange County. According to J. Scott McKibben in *My Town, Your Town—LaGrange—1836–1986*, the Grand Rapids and Indiana Railroad promoted a north and south route through LaGrange as early as 1855. By the time the war had ended, money had been raised and track had been built for the railroad. The first train arrived in LaGrange from Sturgis, Michigan, on April 11, 1870. A station was built on East Spring Street near Fly Creek. The government operated the railroads during World War I. Afterwards, the Pennsylvania Railroad took over the G.R. & I.

The St. Joseph Valley Railroad, known as the Valley Line, was an interurban system that started in Elkhart. Stops along the way were Bristol, Middlebury, Shipshewana, LaGrange, Mongo, Orland, Lake Gage, Angola, and Columbia, Ohio. When the owner, H. E. Bucklin, wealthy manufacturer of Bucklin's Arnica Salve, died, the railroad was put into receivership. It was sold for scrap in 1918. All that remains is the depot on Detroit Street that houses the LaGrange Chamber of Commerce in 1995.

The Pennsylvania Railroad (the old G.R. & I.) likewise declined. On December 24, 1954, the passenger and mail train ran for the last time. The business continued freight service until 1974. In 1977, the tracks and ties were sold and removed.

Businesses had been built along the railroad tracks during its heyday due to the ease of transportation. The Farm Bureau Co-op,

Civil War veteran James Harvey McKibben was born November 5, 1833, in Richland County, Ohio. He enlisted as Private in Company "G," 88th Regiment, Indiana Volunteer Infantry, while living in LaGrange County, and was discharged three years later as Sergeant. He fought at Perryville, Chickamauga, Mission Ridge, and the Atlanta Campaign. He returned to farming and died in 1908. He was the fourth son of James and Sarah McKibben. Courtesy of J. Scott McKibben.

Bert Hart, second from left, was Section Foreman for forty-three years on the Pennsylvania Railroad. Photo 1914; courtesy of his daughter, Lela Stanner.

The Black & White Dining Car was a restaurant run by Mrs. John Woodworth on the east side of Detroit Street, LaGrange. It used to be Car 171 on the St. Joe Valley Line Railroad. It was torn down in 1953. Elster photo; courtesy of Margie Frost.

"Pappy" Elliott is pushing the mail cart to St. Joe Valley Station. He is in front of Elmer Street's house on Detroit Street sometime between 1905 and 1918. Courtesy of Irene Babcock and J. Scott McKibben.

On June 26, 1907, Train 4 of the St. Joe Valley Line was headed for Lake Gage with the engine running backwards, pulling Car 115. The tender derailed, pulling off the rest. Among twenty-five passengers, there were no injuries. It happened at Dan Long's farm near Pleasant Hill. Courtesy of J. Scott McKibben.

This historical sign and new little station mark the site of a stop for the Valley Line Railroad known as Yoder Station. It is located on the Clay Township farm presently owned by Carl Dintaman. Courtesy of Carl Dintaman.

the Home Grain Elevator, and Brady's Stockyards were among them. The pickle factory, run by Verne Beaty, was situated along the west side of the tracks near the corner of Ryason and Walnut Streets. On the east side of the tracks was the stockyards. Pickles and pigs!

W. Verne Beaty was the son of Warren Samuel and Martha Alice (Norris) Beaty. His siblings were Bruce, Sam, Fred, Bess, Goldie, and Pearl. He married Myrta Morrison. Their children were Paul, Raphael, Donald, Alice, and Ruth.

Mr. Beaty started the pickle factory in the mid 1920s. He had other stations in Sturgis and Bronson, Michigan. The pickles were sent to the company of Lutz-Schramm, which paid him three dollars per day when he first began the operation. This was a good wage for the times.

Local growers contracted with Beaty. He provided a pound of seed for each acre of pickles to be planted. His daughter, Ruth, remembers going to the doors of customers' houses and saying, "Here's your seed." Only a certain kind of pickles were desired. That is why seeds were delivered.

In a letter written during World War I to Wilbur Connelly, a soldier from Bloomfield Township, George Olds wrote, "Pickles were fine this year. I made $185 off 1 1/4 acres and picked them all myself."

The growers were paid three dollars for one hundred pounds of "little tinies" or one dollar for one hundred pounds of dill pickle size. Mr. Beaty always made a barrel of dill pickles out of the big ones that could not be sold—free to munch on for those customers who brought in pickles. Neighbors also came to get oversized cucumbers to make their own pickles or relish.

Ford Meyers was the right-hand man who worked steadily in the summer to help sort and salt down pickles. During the harvest, cars would line up in long lines, carrying pickles in all kinds of

The old frame Presbyterian Church, built in 1853, was the first church building in LaGrange. In 1910, Clyde Walb purchased it and converted it into a repair shop for his dredges. It still stands on Factory Street, west of the "1886 House." Yoder photo.

containers. The pickles were sorted on a machine and stored in big vats of salt brine. During periods of long storage, someone had to keep the vats stirred to prevent scum from forming.

Workers used dip nets to remove pickles from the vats, put them in a wheelbarrow, take them up a gangplank, and dump them in vats on the railroad car. Each car had three or four vats that held five hundred to six hunded bushels. By working hard, two people could load a car in one day. The total wage, split between the two workers, was thirty-five dollars by the 1940s.

According to one of the boys who loaded pickles for him, Verne Beaty always went barefoot because there was a lot of water everywhere. The boy said that Verne could pinch a person with his toes harder than most people could pinch with their fingers.

Bill Fegley, retired mail carrier for the town of LaGrange, managed the pickle factory in its final years during the 1950s. It was located in the vicinity of the present-day Dometic plant.

Pluma (Morrison) Dorsey, with stylish hair and gown, lived south of LaGrange on State Road 9. Photo circa 1880 or 1890; courtesy of J. Scott McKibben.

A gas lamp is shown on Detroit Street in LaGrange, prior to electric lights and prior to 1908 when the street was paved with bricks. Note signs for Allen White Drugs & Groceries and the Standard Office. Courtesy of Marian Deal.

In 1913, pioneer Shedrick Carney's grandson, Rollin Carney Sr. (also grandson of pioneers Jacob and Susan Rowan) and his wife, Ada Caldwell (granddaughter of Jacob and Jane Fisher Camp), operated an ice cream parlor on Detroit Street in the building presently occupied by photographer Monty Glick. Customers could "cool off, eat under the palm trees and try our Sweet Heart's Delight, 10 cents. Full line of Chocolates and Bon Bons." Courtesy of Margie Frost.

Built in 1874–1876, the LaGrange School used to stand at the corner of Mountain Street and U.S. 20. The last class graduated in 1964. An apartment building is there now. Gifford photo; courtesy of Margie Frost.

Myrta Sams (Mrs. Don Nelson, 1886–1939), was born on "the knobs" to Dennis and Caroline (Yergin) Sams. She attended the old Minnich School, LaGrange High School, and Albion College (journalism). A. F. Clark photo; courtesy of Myrta's daughter, Irene Babcock.

Ohio natives Charles Large (1839–1901) and Ellen Johnson (1840–1928) were married in Dekalb County, Indiana, in 1861. He made an iron trivet and carved a rolling pin and butter bowl for his bride. He was a blacksmith and carpenter. They moved to Walnut Street in LaGrange where he died in 1901 and she in 1928. Courtesy of granddaughter Lela Stanner.

A Case plow exhibit was held at LaGrange on November 12, 1913. The LaGrange Hardware Company was a local dealer. Gifford photo; J. Scott McKibben collection.

Left
LaGrange resident Robert Will posed for this picture circa 1912. Courtesy of J. Scott McKibben.

Corn School in LaGrange features a merry-go-round. Photo circa 1910–1915; Miles and Judy Perkins collection.

Ray Fisher, on left, is standing with the driver of White's Grocery huckster wagon in front of Fred J. "Brown's Drug" store and across from the LaGrange courthouse (circa 1910–1917). Brown's became a Rexall store in 1910. John Haglind's Real Estate and Insurance sign is to the rear. Rex Fisher collection.

Gypsies could usually be seen at Corn School fairs in the early days. Fortunetelling was popular. Photo circa 1915–1920; Miles and Judy Perkins collection.

This aerial view of LaGrange was taken during Corn School circa 1919 at an elevation of 1,200 feet. Note the carnival rides blocking Detroit Street. Photo by Elster, Howe, Indiana; Perkins collection.

This unidentified man on the horse is facing an old wagon with wooden wheels and pigeon houses in the background. Photo circa 1910; Rowe collection; courtesy of Kathryn Bloom.

Howard Zimmerman and his sister, Ellen Robbins, are seated in the carriage in front of the house he bought in the 1890s for $450. Standing is Ellen's daughter, Willowdean Robbins. Zimmerman was a paperhanger who raised bees. The house is now the home of John and Wilma (Wurtsbaugh) Ellis at 214 North Sherman Street, LaGrange. Ellis collection.

Circa 1913–1914, this farm on "the knobs" was the home of Caroline (Yergin) Butler (widow of Dennis Sams), her second husband, George Butler, and their family. It belonged to George and Nellie Forker later. It is the current home of Jerry and Anneliese Grogg. Drake Studio photo; courtesy of Caroline's granddaughter, Irene Babcock.

This team of threshers appears to be ready for a hard day's work. LaGrange County Historical Society collection.

Irene Nelson (later Mrs. Clark Babcock) is all dressed up in a red velvet outfit with crocheted lace trim and high button shoes. Her grandmother (father Don Nelson's step-mother) made the clothes. She remembers standing on a bench to have her picture taken. Gifford photo, circa 1913 or 1914; Babcock collection.

This couple is set to travel the country in their early camper. Connelly collection.

Caton Brothers Furniture & Undertaking began business around 1908 and stayed in business into the 1960s. It changed to Caton & Frurip Funeral Home and then Caton & Diggins Furniture. Caton's horse-drawn hearse is shown here. J. Scott McKibben collection.

An early Harley Davidson motorcycle with sidecar holds three comfortably. Wilbur Connelly, who lived on "the knobs," is the man in the middle. Photo circa 1916; Connelly collection.

In 1923, Rollin Carney Sr. established the Carney Funeral Home on North Detroit Street along with a furniture store. The funeral home moved to West Michigan (1934–1938), East Michigan (1938–1956), and finally South Detroit Street where it operates as the Carney-Frost Funeral Home. Sons Frank, Willard, and Rollin Jr. and Gordon Frost, grandson, joined the firm over the years. Carney's hearse is pictured on West Michigan Street. Frost collection.

Elmer Pfaff had a barber shop on Detroit Street for many years, and his wife, "Georgie," had a beauty shop. The big snow picture was taken February 1, 1939, where the Sportsman is now located. Courtesy of Kathryn Bloom.

Verne Schlemmer (left) and his brother, Don, are waiting for self-serve customers to bring items to the counter of Schlemmer Brothers' Hardware on Detroit street. December 1956 photo; Schlemmer collection.

Irene Nelson is sitting on a Dodge belonging to her future husband, Clark Babcock, parked at John and Grace Babcock's farm (200E 1335S). During World War II, she worked at a defense plant in Indianapolis, but most of her life has been spent in Bloomfield Township where she has worked as a cook, schoolbus driver, and mother to Mary Ann and John. Photo circa 1929; Babcock collection.

The original location of Purity Super Market, Inc. was on the corner of Detroit and Lafayette Streets in downtown LaGrange. Glenn Eash, former sheriff, and wife, Mary, founded the business on January 1, 1949. A new store was built in 1954 at its present Detroit and South Streets location. It has expanded since then. Jim and Nina Eash and sons, Jeffrey and Bradley, joined the firm, too. Photo courtesy of Nina and Jim Eash.

Reed's Service Station was out in the country, two miles west of town on U.S. 20 where Buck Creek crosses the highway. It was originally owned by Eulie Need. It was one of four gas stations built on the same plan in the 1920s. This one sold Phillips 66, two sold Texaco and one sold Cities Service. Dwight Hostetler had one of these stations built at the west edge of town. In 1948, it was bought by Monroe and Nina Walters and moved by Henry Tjarks to its present location on South Detroit Street. A kitchen was built on the back, and it became Walter's Uptown Restaurant. Succeeding owners were John Reed, Jim Hillman, and John Gilmore. It now operates as Mom's Restaurant. Photo circa 1930s; courtesy of Wilma Ellis.

David (1857–1936) and Catherine (Kitty, 1866–1958) Latta, their son, Silas (1891–1927), and their dog are posed in front of their house (on 250W 200N, two miles north of Lambright's Hatchery by today's description) near where Saylor School used to be. Note the twin doors and steps on the left wing. An Amish family lives there now. Photo circa 1906; courtesy of Wilma Ellis.

2

Clay Township

Clay Township was originally surveyed in 1829 and organized on September 4, 1838. Although Clay contains no towns within its boundaries, the east side of the township is connected to the west side of the town of LaGrange.

Buck Lake, on the northern border of the township, was a stopping place for the Indians on their way back and forth to Goshen. It was a place of beauty.

Deposits of bog-iron ore were extracted from Hobbs' Marsh in the northeastern corner of the township and hauled by wagon a couple of miles to the forge on the Pigeon River, several miles west and south of Lima (*Counties of LaGrange and Noble, Indiana, 1882*).

As the writer (apparently Silas B. McManus) wrote in his occasional column "Old Forge Folk" in the *LaGrange Standard*, "Only one poor old dilapidated, fast-falling-to-pieces building is left on the Old Forge ground by the Pigeon [River] near the [Pigeon] Lake. This is a part of the store building where Enoch Hawk used to keep a stock of goods—a few pieces of calico, a bit of cotton cloth (factory, they called it), some groceries and boots and shoes and, I very distinctly recollect, a big box of alum quite out of proportion to the other supplies. It has been a mystery I have never solved, Why so much alum?"

The columnist described the joy and fury of the hoedowns given in the storeroom and yearned for the folks that used to live at the Old Forge "down there by the river, the air quivering with the throb of the great bellows, or shattered to shreds by the beat of the trip hammer—it was a very simple, primative [*sic*] performance, and yet fair to middling big to the people who lived there then." The ironmaking business became unprofitable just prior to the Civil War and was discontinued.

Some of the early settlers were Madison and Michael Sprague, Thomas and Anson Clark, Erastus Clark, John and Charlotte Ryason, Mr. and Mrs. Montgomery (parents of triplets born circa 1837), Richard Salmon and his father, John Ramsey, Obadiah

James (right), John (center), and Shedrick (left) were sons of Clay Township pioneer Shedrick Carney who was married three times. John (1850–1920) and young Shedrick (1852–1927) were half brothers to James (1840–1916). James served in Company "G," 30th Indiana Volunteers during the Civil War and farmed in Tennessee for several years. He married twice, but had no children. Shedrick Jr. lived in the LaGrange area and fathered William, Albert, and Delbert. John Carney farmed all his life in LaGrange County. He had seven children, Dr. Frank and Rollin Sr. among them. Elster photo; Frost collection.

Lawrence, Elisha Thorp and his three sons, William, John, and Jacob. Daniel Webster once owned land in section nine, but never lived there.

Shedrick Carney was contracted to furnish lumber for the first courthouse in the town of LaGrange at $6.50 per thousand feet. He was paid to clear the town square of trees. He did such a good job that not a tree was left. After the courthouse was built, shade trees had to be planted.

Other early farmers, their dates of settlement and places of origin, were John Roy, 1838, New York; John Robbins, 1836, Pennsylvania; Ira M. Woodworth, 1852, New York; and William Maxwell, 1860, Indiana, but born in Ireland. Many other farmers soon followed.

Samuel Beaty was a cooper who earned enough money from his profession to buy a yoke of oxen which he, in turn, used to clear his farmland. Beaty Township School No. 10 was built on his land in section 33 of Clay Township.

Businessmen who advertised in the atlases were James Kennedy, lumberman, who settled in 1847 from Pennsylvania; Christian Giggy, stone mason, 1865, Switzerland; Christian Plank, "Manufacturer of Fork and Broom Handles and Dealer in Smooth and Rough Lumber," 1862, Pennsylvania; and E. Fleck, "Manufacturer of and Dealer in Flour, Feed, etc. and Dealer in Rough Lumber," Ohio, 1865.

Samuel Hood built a sawmill in 1835–1837 in section 15 on Buck Creek. Levi Knott then ran the mill. According to the history of *LaGrange, 1882,* Emanuel Fleck bought the sawmill site in 1865 and by 1867 had rebuilt the mill.

Many early residents did their trading at Lima. Baubauga Road (county road 50N in 1995) was laid out in 1837 *(LaGrange County Centennial History, 1828–1928).* It became a main route which, in later years, links LaGrange and Shipshewana.

Christian and Ellen Giggy came to Clay Township in the 1850s from Kapallen, Canton of Berne, Switzerland. Christian was a stonemason and farmer. Their children were Charles, Oscar, Mary, Rosanna, and Sarah (Mrs John Fisher, born in 1861). Rex Fisher collection.

This is Carney's yoke of oxen. Which Carney is not certain, but probably the oxen belonged to a descendant of pioneer Shedrick Carney. Courtesy of Rex Fisher; Hilda Hughes collection.

Samuel and Martha (Beidler) Fisher came to Clay Township in 1863 from Tuscarawas County, Ohio. They ran a sawmill and gristmill on Buck Creek with sons-in-law Emanuel Fleck and Jacob Camp. Rex Fisher collection.

Right
A reunion was held at Fisher's Landing at Oliver Lake in Johnson Township on August 29, 1939. Attending (left to right) were Oscar, Sarah, and Charles, children of Christian and Ellen Giggy. Rex Fisher collection.

Three men were killed in 1876 when a steam boiler exploded at the sawmill owned by William Price and Joseph Kennedy, two miles northwest of LaGrange. According to the *Combined Atlases*, those killed were Joseph Kennedy, Sebastian Gross, and Henry Corwin.

David J. Norris came to LaGrange County in 1876 and purchased a farm in Clay Township. In 1890 he became a township trustee. The first district schoolhouse in the county to be heated by a furnace was built by Norris.

The mills continued to serve as magnets for work and socialization. These were places to meet the neighbors, exchange ideas, obtain building materials, and have the grain ground. In 1871, a gristmill was added at Fleck's. It was three and one-half miles northwest of LaGrange.

After Fleck's wife died (Savilla, Samuel Fisher's daughter, who had borne fourteen children), he left for California. In 1886, Samuel Fisher, now seventy-one years old, took control of the grist- and sawmill. After his death in 1890, his son, John Henry Fisher, succeeded him. In 1897, John Henry and wife, Sadie, traveled to Ohio to visit his elderly sisters when disaster struck. On October 9, 1897, the mill caught fire and was destroyed.

Prior to the mill's destruction, ice had been sold from the millpond to LaGrange ice men who cut, housed, and later sold the ice to area residents. On February 14, 1899, the *LaGrange Standard* reported, "The headquarters for ice this winter is at Fisher's

John Ford had a tenant farm located by the intersection of Townline Road and Hawpatch. Son of pioneers Jared and Rebecca Ford, he and his wife, Louisa (Price), lived on a farm on the Clay Township side of Townline Road along with their children Myron, Clara (later Mrs Eugene Fisher), and Jared ("Jeddy"). After Jeddy's parents died, guardian Laora Rowe contracted with John Fisher to farm the property and tend to Jeddy (seated at left), a grown man who needed care. Jeddy's house was on the east side of the road. Photo circa 1908; Rex Fisher collection.

LANDING
DRINK
Coca-Cola

Mary Seaney took this parlor picture of the farmhouse on Baubauga Road on March 4, 1916 (She was a seventh and eighth grade teacher at Lima School). The angel table (brass angels are attached to each side of the table), piano and bench, spindle rocking chair, and two pictures are still in family possession. On the left is a charcoal drawing of Mrs. Thomas (Mary Ann Molleston) Seaney (1831–1900). The other picture shows Bertha Ramsay (later Mrs. T. H. Seaney) and her pupils in front of Hoagland School near Fort Wayne in the early 1890s. Rex Fisher collection.

This Victorian home once belonged to L. and Mary Showalter whose daughter, Sophia, and fiancé Herman Sigrist of Brighton, had an elaborate wedding on June 15, 1905. Located on Baubauga Road, one and one-half miles west of LaGrange, it featured a tower with widow's walk, and lattice work. It became home to Thomas and Bertha (Ramsay) Seaney in 1910. Their children were Roy, Mary, and Clarence. Oscar Christner owned the farm later. Jacob Schrock, an Amish man, and his family live there now. In 1992, they removed the tower, which had squirrels in it. Rex Fisher collection.

An unidentified man is standing beside part of some dredging equipment. Clay Township was dredged in 1916. Driving and riding horses are sheltered under the trees. LaGrange County Historical Society collection.

The LaGrange County Infirmary (later Mark's Nursing Home) housed the poor of the county. The main building was erected in 1883, one-half mile west of LaGrange. A year later, on February 28, the *LaGrange Standard* gave this obituary:

Little Mary Brown, aged 7 years, an inmate of the County House, died of lung fever week before last and her little form was carried over the hill from the poor house to her last resting place in the corner of the farm where the dead of the County House are buried.

An elderly occupant made the tombstones from concrete and artifacts such as jars, lids, china, shells, etc. to mark the graves of people, and perhaps even animals, who lived on the county farm. No names or dates were applied. Only one government headstone for a Civil War veteran is marked. Who could be lying beneath this stone with a toy gun embedded in it? The cemetery grounds are now a part of the LaGrange Country Club grounds. Yoder photo, 1995.

millpond. There are probably 50 tons taken away every day. The quality of ice is good."

In February 1898, the old dam at the millpond washed out, taking with it a large quantity of ice that LaGrange partners Sitler and Devlin had cut but not housed. Since the John H. Fishers had been forced to sell the farm after the fire, the new owners decided not to rebuild the dam but to farm the additional acres. Sitler and his partner, Thomas K. Devlin, then turned to Oliver Lake for their ice supply (*LaGrange Standard*). Following their financial loss, John and Sadie (Sarah R. Giggy) Fisher became tenant farmers on the John R. Ford farm in Clay Township. In 1920 they bought a twenty-acre farm on Seminary Road (later U.S. 20), half a mile west of LaGrange. Sadie was, according to her grandchildren, the best baker of sour cream sugar cookies there ever was. John Henry died in 1932 and Sadie in 1940. Their small farm has remained in the family and, according to her grandson, Rex Fisher, "Sadie's pie safe, built by John Henry, in which she kept her sour cream sugar cookies, remains in the basement where it has been since the 1920s. But, alas, it contains no cookies, just memories."

Clay Township was settled by a mixture of people, mainly from the eastern states, many of whom have descendants living in the area even today. There are still no towns, but the people live together as a community, farming, or working in nearby towns.

These 1921 photos show Chester Wurtsbaugh on the Zimmerman farm one and one-half miles west of LaGrange on Baubauga Road (50N). He is shown with his Ford sedan and a Gurnsey cow. Horse Belle is in the background. Wilma Ellis collection.

Chester Wurtsbaugh worked at this sawmill (name and location uncertain) in 1921–1922. Wilma Ellis collection.

These school children likely attended Saylor School, located two and one-half miles west and two and one-half miles north of LaGrange. They are Woodrow, Thelma, Sambo, Leroy, Grace, and Donald. Surnames were not recorded. Wilma Ellis collection.

These Saylor School children were sledding. Their white wooden school has been torn down since then. Photo circa 1920s; Wilma Ellis collection.

The first graders are lined up in front of Green School, District No 6 in section 21. Marion Atwater is second from left and Verne Schlemmer is fourth from left. Other members of the class in random order are Rosalie Anspaugh, Ruth Mishler, Marguerite Connelly, Mae Schrock, Margaret Doney, Zola Schrock, Ernest Gooch, Charles Woodworth, Roy Foltz, and John Campbell. This was the largest class in the school There was a total of thirty-eight pupils, with none in the second and sixth grades and only one in the eighth. Irma Miller taught them all. Walter Atwater was Trustee and Hilda Hughes was County Superintendent. Photo 1925; Verne Schlemmer collection.

Forest and Woodrow are crosscut sawing circa 1920s. Wilma Ellis collection.

Right
LaGrange County is a land of lakes, but Clay Township has only one—Buck Lake. In 1942, Rex Fisher, age ten, took his bamboo pole with hook, bobber, and fishworms, and went fishing at the gravel pit on Buck Creek, which drains from the lake. It was on the Burt and Lou (Latta) Walter farm two miles west of LaGrange on U.S. 20. When the bobber bobbed, Rex whipped the pole over his head. Out of the water a fish came flying, arced over his head, flew off the hook, and landed on the bank behind him. It was a trout, thirteen and one-half inches long and weighing one and one-half pounds. He ran to the kitchen to show everyone. Grandma Walters approved, but was relieved when the wiggling fish was removed from over her lunch table. Rex Fisher collection.

This goat named Spot and four sows are on the Howard Zimmerman farm on Baubauga Road in Clay Township where Chester Wurtsbaugh lived. Photo 1944; Wilma Ellis collection.

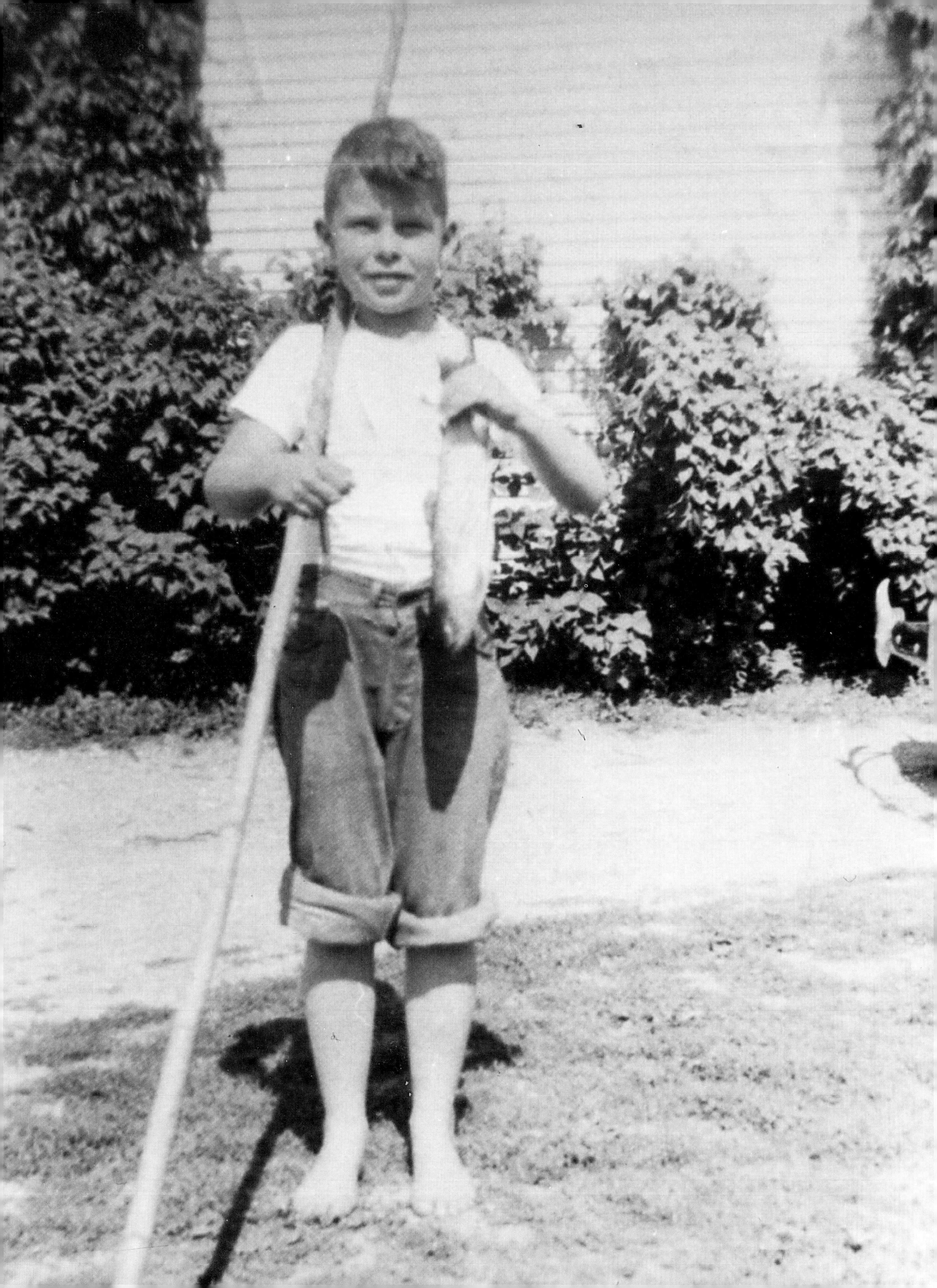

This view, from Rogers Park looking south, is of the original clear spring and the Roy homestead site. Part of the white house used to be a wayside inn. Ervin and Arlene Mullet and their family live here now. Yoder photo, 1995.

3

Clearspring Township

Anthony Nelson was the first person to enter land in the area that became Clearspring Township. Originally from Ohio, he moved to Elkhart County in 1829 and then to LaGrange County. In 1832 he entered three eighty-acre lots. He still has descendants in LaGrange County. Among them is Glen W. Smith, his great-grandson. According to Smith, Nelson paid $1.25 an acre for the land which is one and one-half miles north of present-day Topeka. There were no townships then. He built his house in the middle of two of these plats, and when the townships were platted, his house was in the middle of the road.

He was hired to build a road from Howe to Ligonier. Hawpatch Road is part of this road. Nelson and his men camped out on the job all summer, says Smith, who grew up on part of his great-grandfather's land. Glen W. Smith has always lived in and near Topeka and will soon be ninety years old.

Dr. David Rogers was an herb doctor from Geneva, New York. In 1833 he entered 1,280 acres. His grave is on his land which today is Rogers Park, operated by the LaGrange County Parks Department.

Charles and Jane (Oliver) Roy moved from New York State to LaGrange County in June 1836 in a covered wagon. They settled on land they purchased by labor from Dr. Rogers. They built their log cabin near a spring called Clearspring; it was from the spring that the Roy farm, Clearspring Farm, and the township were named. It was a well-known spot for Indians and settlers to stop for a cold drink. Several other springs were located there, too.

Other newcomers were John S. Gibson, 1835, section 33; E. Schermerhorn who left New York in 1836 and arrived in LaGrange County in 1840, section 4; Richard Green, 1844, section 35; Nicholas Low; and Hawley Peck, 1838, from Connecticut (he moved onto his land in 1846). Orin Kent came to Clearspring from Connecticut at an early date, but he did not settle his land until later (*Combined Atlases*). In 1837, LaGrange County commissioners

Anthony Nelson was the first person to buy land in Clearspring Township in 1832. Photo courtesy of great-grandson, Glen Smith.

David Rogers Park contains several log houses moved to the site and restored. Dr. David Rogers died in 1871, willing his estate to the orphans and needy children of the county. As a result, the Rogers Orphans Home was built on section 22. Later, the orphanage and farm were both sold except for fifteen acres. The proceeds were put in a fund to carry out his wishes. The park on the remaining land, containing his grave and a memorial shaft as well as the historical buildings, remains for the education and recreation of the county. David Rogers Days is held annually at the park where stories, music, crafts, and foods of yesteryear can be enjoyed. Yoder photo, 1995.

divided Eden Township, leaving the western half as Eden and naming the eastern half Clearspring.

Additional farmers, dates of settlement, and origins were: Celia Butler, 1846, Virginia; L. Dallas, Samuel Dallas, and Levi Dallas, 1836, Ohio; George W. Doe, 1852, Ohio; Solomon Fleck, 1847, Ohio; Ira Ford, 1856, New York; John Greenawalt, 1854, Ohio; William H. Hoverstock, 1844, Ohio; Isaac Hoerner, 1849, Ohio; George Harwood, 1845, Indiana; Jacob Harshberger, 1865, Pennsylvania; William H. Hall, 1853, Indiana; I. S. Jones, 1836, New York; David Kurtz, 1851, Pennsylvania; William T. Nelson, 1845, Indiana; M. J. Nelson, 1832, Indiana; William T. Parks, 1835, Ohio; A. H. Price, 1846, Ohio; Leonard Peck, 1845, New York; William H. Price, 1847, Maryland; Solomon Ritter, 1846, Pennsylvania; Frank W. Row, 1854, Indiana; James Smith; George B. Ulmer, 1852, Indiana; C. W. Weatherwax, 1858, Michigan; Charles Wolf, 1867, New York; David Yoder, 1864, Pennsylvania; J. J. Yoder, 1864, Ohio; and W. Yarwood, 1860, England (*Combined Atlases*).

In October 1861, John J. Gillette joined Company "H," 44th Indiana Volunteers, under the leadership of Capt. (later Major) William B. Bingham. He served in the Civil War for three years. Afterward, he farmed Richard Green's farm and taught school. He married Jennie M. Church, and they had two children, Grace and Almon. The Gillettes moved to a farm near Wolcottville in 1877.

This monument at Shiloh National Military Park honors the 44th Indiana Volunteer Infantry. Companies of this regiment were raised in the Tenth Congressional District. Hugh B. Reed was its colonel. All the men of Company "H" were from LaGrange County. At Shiloh, 33 men were killed and 177 wounded from the regiment. Yoder photo, 1995.

John Gillette (1842–1927) was a member of the Grand Army of the Republic. His picture is on a reunion badge for the 44th Indiana Volunteer Infantry. It is part of the collection of William Opie, Sergeant of Company "D," Milford Township. This collection has been given to the LaGrange County Historical Society, Inc. Gillette later served as Worthy Master of the Pixley Grange of the Patrons of Husbandry. Courtesy of LaGrange County Historical Society.

Mr. Gillette later served two terms as county auditor (*Combined Atlases*).

James Dallas, another Civil War soldier, was born in Clearspring Township February 16, 1845. He enlisted in the 44th Indiana Volunteer Infantry, October 1862, and was honorably discharged May 2, 1863. He reenlisted in the 12th Indiana Cavalry January 2, 1864, and mustered out in December, 1865 (*Combined Atlases*). He, like Gillette, also moved to Johnson Township later.

Another long-time Clearspring resident was Clark F. Todd, born March 14, 1844, in Lima Township, to Joseph and Catharine Todd (who came from Seneca County, Ohio). Clark joined Company "B," 12th Regiment of Indiana Volunteer Infantry on August 11, 1862.

The Clark and Maria Todd family posed for this picture in 1914. They are second and third from the left in the middle row. Connelly collection.

Prisoner of War Records show that his regiment participated in the battle of Richmond where 173 were killed and wounded. The Colonel died of his wounds. They had been sent to Kentucky to resist the invasion of Kirby Smith. Most of the regiment, including Private Todd, were captured on August 30, 1862, and afterward exchanged as prisoners of war. He later served at Camp Sherman, Mississippi, and Scottsboro, Alabama. War Records also indicate that he was a patient in a Memphis, Tennessee, hospital due to illness. He participated in the siege of Vicksburg and the march to the sea. The regiment took part in the Atlanta Campaign, participating in the battles at Dallas, Resacca, New Hope Church, Kennesaw Mountain, Jonesboro, and many skirmishes. From November 14 to December 10, 1864, it marched with Sherman's army from Atlanta to the sea at Savannah. He was discharged at Washington, D.C. on June 8, 1865, by reason of the close of the war. The following year, he married Maria Angeline Eagleton, who had been born in Milan, Ohio, to Joseph and ? (Bills) Eagleton. Clark and Maria (pronounced with a long *i*) moved to Clearspring Township, section 14.

After the Civil War ended, many brick homes and business districts were built throughout the county. In Clearspring Township, business increased. The "Business Directory for the Cities and Villages of LaGrange County," in the 1874 atlas, lists the following people in Clearspring Township: E. Nelson, farmer and trustee; Willard Hervey, farmer and Justice of the Peace; Silas B. Peck, farmer and blacksmith; N. Babcock, farmer and teacher; Henry J. Ulmer, farmer and brickmaker; and Willian D. Sloan, a blacksmith.

Haw Patch (now Topeka) was platted in Clearspring Township on December 9, 1871, in the northwest part of section 31 by Joseph Kinney and twenty-six others. The part of town first called Topeka is situated in the northeast part of section 36 in Eden Township. It was laid out by the Indiana Improvement Company, June 14, 1893, according to the *History of Northeast Indiana, Vol. I.* Thus, the present town of Topeka is in both Clearspring and Eden townships.

The only villages in Clearspring Township are Topeka and Eddy. Eddy is a spot in the road where a railway siding was built in section 35, a mile west of Atwood Lake. Neat farmsteads can be seen, but no actual village is discernible now.

Topeka was formerly called Haw Patch because of the profusion of hawthornes that grew throughout the area. Even more commonly, the village was called Slabtown because its sawmills and houses were made of slabwood. In 1893, when the Wabash Railroad was built, the name was changed to Topeka because of its similarities to Topeka, Kansas *(History of Northeast Indiana, Vol. I).*

According to *Celebrating a Century 1893–1993* by the Topeka Area Historical Society, Beulah Church was dedicated in May 1881 by the Evangelical Union Mennonites on land in section 21 of Clearspring Township. John Greenwalt deeded the land to this group with the stipulation that it should also be free to other denominations. If they stopped using the land, it was to go to another Christian church. The Methodists bought the church later. The last service was in 1946. Robert Thompson owns the land. Yoder photo, 1995.

Sand Hill School was built on section 12 on Mahlon Strickland's land. It was later moved three-fourths mile west onto Solomon Harding's land in section 11, Hawpatch Road. It is no longer used as a school, but school was still held there in the 1950s. Yoder photo, 1995.

right
The children of Elias and Katherine (Medlem) Olinghouse are Martha (standing), Mrs. Benjamin Franklin Dovel, 1882–1939; twins Ray (left), 1892–1962, who married Emma Bowen; and Roy (center), 1892–1935, who married Leta Trittipo; and Russell (right), 1890–1981, who married Neva Norris and later Bessie Stewart. Another daughter, Mary (1877–1883), had already died. Photo 1892; courtesy of Janice Olinghouse Keller.

This steam-powered road grader is being operated two and one-half miles east of Topeka by (left to right) Burt Jones, a township employee, and Russell, Ray, and Roy Olinghouse (sons of Elias and Katherine). It is believed that Russell or Ray owned the engine and probably their father did before them. The family interest in steam threshing continues today into the fifth generation. Russell and Neva Olinghouse had two children, Wayne of LaGrange, and Geraldine (Leeper) of Bremen. Russell owned a Case and later a Russell engine. Roy and his wife had three children. Ray and his wife had eight children, among them Mildred (Mrs. Woodrow Hostetler of Shipshewana). Ray owned a threshing rig from 1919 to 1935 in the Atwood Lake area. He favored Avery steam engines. R. M. Hawkins photo (Benton Harbor, Michigan), circa 1920; Keller collection.

Sycamore Literary Hall was built in Topeka on the east side of the main street in Clearspring Township in 1905. It accidentally burned on April 16, 1915, and was rebuilt immediately. It served the community well for many years for graduations, plays, etc. In 1967, the last graduation was held there. Westview School Corporation began the next year and the building fell into disrepair. It was demolished in 1980. Courtesy of Richard Marks.

These are first grade pupils at Pixley School, located one-half mile south and one-half mile west of the Rogers Home, in 1922. They are (left to right) unknown, Bruce Taylor, unknown, Clara (Roy) Hirschy, Sterling Hostetler, Vivian (Ulmer) Smith, Irlin Ulmer, Jemima (Yoder) Gingrich, Wilford Hostetler, and Dorothy (Wemple) Myers. Courtesy of Clara Hirschy.

This is the Byron Price home one mile north and three miles east of Topeka. Price went to Pixley School all eight years. According to *Celebrating a Century*, he was president of the Gridiron Club in Washington, in charge of the Associated Press offices in Washington, Director of Censorship, and Assistant Secretary General of the United Nations. He was a Topeka High School graduate, class of 1908, and a graduate of Wabash College. Courtesy of Clara Hirschy.

Amish farm animals cluster together on a late winter day. Yoder photo, 1995.

The Emma Store was originally built in 1881 by Jacob and Andrew Hostetler. Other owners followed. This store burned, so the new brick one seen here was built in 1931. Howard and Evelyn Fought operated it from 1938 to 1981. It was sold to Richard and Myrna Gerber who ran it until 1989. It was closed for a while, but has been reopened since then. Yoder photo, 1995.

The Honeyville General Store was established in 1850. It burned in 1902, according to *Celebrating a Century,* and was rebuilt the next year. It was closed from 1965 to 1980, but has reopened to serve the tourists and local residents. Old shelving and counters from the Haggerty Brothers Store in Scott and a wooden cooler and showcases add to the quaint atmosphere. Yoder photo, 1995.

4

Eden Township

On November 5, 1832, Eden Township became the third township in LaGrange County. It was separated from Lima Township, which had comprised the western half of the county. William McConnell and Robert Latta were the first settlers. Latta's home became a gathering place for fellow Methodists. He donated land to build the first Methodist church in the township, Eden Chapel. It was organized in 1835 and built in 1842. William McConnell entered land in a section adjoining Latta's. Both men at one time owned eighteen "eighties."

Eden was a place of beauty, named for the biblical Garden of Eden. The Haw Patch, within it, was an area free of underbrush and stones, containing rich black soil and black haw bushes, and covered by a carpet of wildflowers.

Mrs. Elizabeth Ramsby, her five sons, and two daughters came in 1834 from Ohio; William Parks, 1834; and John Thompson, 1835, from Ohio. Thompson settled in the center of Haw Patch in an area still known as Thompson's Corners. A schoolhouse at the corners bore his name. From 1856 to 1860, he was a state senator for which he received three dollars per day. He went back and forth from home to the state capitol on horseback. Mrs. Glen W. Knauss of LaGrange was his great-granddaughter (*LaGrange Centennial*).

Nehemiah Coldren arrived in VanBuren Township in 1829 from Pennsylvania and settled in Eden Township in 1836. He was the first sheriff of LaGrange County. He received this appointment in 1830 from the governor of Indiana. Coldren's oldest daughter was the first female white child born in LaGrange County.

In 1837 the John Dennys built a hewn log house, two miles west of present-day Topeka and one-half mile south. Walter Denny, father of John, lived with the family, too. He was a Revolutionary soldier who was with Washington at Valley Forge and crossed the Delaware with him (*LaGrange Centennial*). Among the early settlers were James Taylor, 1837; William Hoverstock, 1840; Nicholas Lowe, 1840; Catherine Miller, 1838; William Collett, 1836; Robert

Civil War soldier Andrew Hart belonged to Company "H," 44th Regiment of Indiana Volunteers. He gave his age as nineteen. He died on January 20, 1862, at a hospital in Henderson, Kentucky. Cause of death was typhoid fever or measles, depending on the source consulted. Photo circa 1861; Lela (Hart) Stanner collection.

Top right
Amish buggies and a church wagon (which holds benches used for seating during church services held at one another's homes) are parked at a home on State Road 5 in Eden Township one Sunday morning in the spring of 1995. Yoder photo.

Bottom right
These horses and buggies are on a Topeka street. One of them is pulling a wagon loaded with boards. Yoder photo, 1995.

McKibben, 1836; and Norman J. Babcock, representative for the district. Babcock was a teacher and public speaker, often on agricultural topics. He was instrumental in the founding of Sycamore Literary Hall (*LaGrange Centennial*). Peter Huser settled on the northwest corner of section 21. Although his eighty acres were in Eden Township, his post office address was Ligonier. David Shoup came from Pennsylvania in 1854 (*Combined Atlases*).

Other settlers were David Sutton, William Denny, William Poyser, Abiah R. Zook, Samuel B. Showalter, M. J. Nelson, John S. Ramsby, Andrew Funk, Eli Parks, John D. Zook, John B. Brant, Milton Rowe, Eden Craig, Samuel J. Hostetler, and Jonathan J. Olinghouse. Orin Kent and family came from Ohio. His son, Robert, served in the Civil War in Company "B," 12th Cavalry, 127th Regiment of the Indiana Volunteers. Robert was also a trustee of Eden Township for two terms. David J. Hartzler was an Amish Mennonite settler. Nathan Kent and his wife, Josie (Coldren), owned a farm in Eden Township. Mr. Kent was a township trustee for two terms and also served as the county assessor.

In 1871 Amos Bowser bought a farm in Eden Township. He had served in the Civil War in Company "I," 48th Indiana Volunteer Infantry. He was in the siege of Vicksburg, the Atlanta Campaign, and Sherman's march through Georgia. He married Clara Poyser, daughter of William Poyser.

No history of the Eden-Clearspring-Newbury areas can be told without mentioning the arrival of the Amish Mennonites. In a little book (twenty pages) with a lengthy title (*A History of the First Settlers of the Amish Mennonites and the Establishment of Their First Congregation in the State of Indiana, Along With a Short Account of the Division Which Took Place in This Church*), Hans Borntreger wrote an account, in 1907, of the first settlement of Amish Mennonites in Indiana. According to him, twenty-four persons left Somerset County, Pennsylvania, in June 1841, to find a new home. Among them were Daniel S. Miller and Christian Bontrager who settled in Newbury Township in the fall. In October 1841, the Emanuel Millers came to LaGrange County from Ohio. The first worship service was held at Daniel Miller's home in the fall of 1841. The following spring, eight more families came to LaGrange County from Somerset County, Pennsylvania. They were the elderly Abraham Hershbergers, Joseph and John Hershbergers, Henry and John Millers, Philip Weiricks, Christian Hochstetlers, and David Lehmanns. Many others followed.

The church was split into the Clinton District and the LaGrange District in 1847 due to growth. According to the *Combined Atlases*, the Amish Church was organized at Haw Patch in 1854.

The Amish and Mennonite people make up a large portion of the western part of LaGrange County today. The Amish broke away from the original Mennonite sect in the seventeenth century and formed their own church. (See the Newbury Township chapter for more information about the Mennonites.)

In section 9 is the only other village in Eden Township other than the western part of Topeka. Originally, it was called Shrock, the name of the post office. Amos and John Shrock owned most of

HONEYVILLE FEED SERVICE

the land thereabout. There was a mill at Shrock and a tile factory nearby. Also, a soap factory is marked on the 1874 map of section 8 of Shrock's land. The name was changed later to Honeyville. Today there is a feed mill, a school, a general store, and Honeyville Metal Works, Inc.

When Eden Township was first settled, there were numerous wetlands. Today there are laws protecting these areas as a refuge for wildlife and as a vital part of the environment. In the latter part of the nineteenth century and the beginning of the twentieth, citizens were primarily concerned with clearing as much farmland as possible. This meant chopping down trees, burning undergrowth, and draining, tiling, and dredging wetlands. Today, people are beginning to realize that these methods of "reclamation" were too harsh and led to the relocation, extinction, or reduction of many species of plants and animals.

Prior to 1874, a two-mile-long State Ditch had been dug in Eden Township. An additional ditch was dug running north and south. Many ditches were begun in 1881 when a new ditch law was passed. In July 1884, Fly Creek was ditched (mainly in Bloomfield Township). By 1893, Eden Township also had Eden-Rowe, Bowen, Harter, Emmitto, Eden, and Gary ditches (*Combined Atlases*).

Dredging was big business. The most successful dredger in the county was Clyde A. Walb. The son of Clay Township farmer, Reuben Walb, Clyde taught in Clay schools and at Wolcottville before spending six years as LaGrange County Surveyor, an elective office. In 1907 he entered the dredging business in a big way. He secured major contracts in Indiana and the Midwest. In LaGrange

Top right
Honeyville School was built in 1930 to consolidate the Eden Township schools for grades one through nine. It now holds students from kindergarten through fourth grade. The school, part of Westview School Corporation, has recently won acclaim for the excellence of its educational program and the high achievement of its students. Yoder photo, 1995.

Bottom right
Orla and Mary Schlabach and sons own Honeyville Feed Service, Inc. Wolf Grain Company and Eli, Freeman, and Wilbur Christners were former owners. The old Honeyville School (formerly Schrock School) is part of the complex at the far left in the picture. Yoder photo, 1995.

This is the Greenwalt dredge on the Rowe Ditch dug by Hostetler and McDonald. LaGrange County Historical Society collection.

Johnathan and Mary (Collett) Olinghouse lived in Eden Township where Johnathan was a blacksmith. Their children were (left to right, front) Theodore, Charles, Elias, and Burther. Back row: Etta, Ada, and Mary. Elias (1853–1936) was a well-known thresher from 1874 to 1914. He bought Frick engines. He moved to Clearspring Township and served as trustee. Photo circa 1880s; Keller collection.

This neat farm extends along the road near the Honeyville General Store. Yoder photo, 1995.

County he won the 1910 contract to dredge Bloomfield's Fly Creek over eighteen other bidders.

In 1916 he won the controversial Clay Township Buck Creek dredging contract. Farmers who "benefited" from the dredging were assessed the costs of the work. Besides managing to pay for the assessment, farmers also had to figure out what to do with the massive mounds of dirt banks, how to get from one side of the ditch to the other, and how to farm the odd shaped pieces of land left behind by the dredge. So much for progress.

The Topeka Depot and Train Museum are pictured to the right of the house. The Topeka Area Historical Society bought the old Wabash Depot, which had closed in 1979, from Norfolk and Western Railroad, raising the money from 1988 to 1990. A section of track was laid and a caboose was leased from the Elkhart New York Central Museum. It was moved to the site in 1992. Yoder photo, 1995.

The Topeka elevator used to overlook the Wabash Railroad tracks where grain was shipped out in closed train cars. Norfolk and Western took over in 1964, but stopped serving Topeka in the late 1970s and early 1980s. The tracks were removed in 1985. Yoder photo, 1995.

Emma School, Twp. No. 1, was built on Moses Hostetler's land in section 1. Located west of Emma, it is now Leonard Lambright's granary. Yoder photo, 1995.

Following page
The public landing at Emma Lake is a popular spot for local people to launch their fishing boats. Yoder photo, 1995.

Greenfield Mills, Inc., is operated by Howard and Helen Lee Rinkel and their son, Dan, and daughter, Joyce. Tours are available on Tuesdays and Thursdays by appointment. Yoder photo, 1995.

5

Greenfield Township

Many of the early settlers of Greenfield Township lived first in Michigan. Several lived near White Pigeon. Michigan land was heavily forested and hard to clear. When the pioneers heard that Indiana land in what is now Greenfield Township had prairies that were ready to be plowed, they took up claims. Among the first to establish claims on Pretty and English Prairies in 1829 were Amos Barr, William Miller, and Benjamin Jones. The latter two moved near the future site of Lexington, later called Brighton (*LaGrange, 1882*).

By 1830, other families settled on the prairies of Greenfield: Thomas Burnell, John Emerson, John Olney, Mr. Sutford, Jesse Huntsman, Felix Miller, James Miller, Jesse Champlin, Samuel Anderson, Ephraim Seeley, J. Croy, and Mr. Wolgamott. Others quickly followed until the prairie land was claimed. The first election in Greenfield Township was held in October 1831 (*Combined Atlases*). By 1832, twenty-five or more families lived in the township. The squatters rushed to buy the land they had settled once it came on the market.

Indians were still living in this area. According to the history of *LaGrange, 1882,* during the summer of the Blackhawk War, 1832, residents were afraid that bands of local Indians might "rise up" against them. Feeding on these fears, three or four men at a northern Springfield mill (a part of Greenfield Township until May 1834, when Springfield and Greenfield became separate townships) talked with customers Gage and Langdon until late at night about the possibility of an attack. The other men decided to play a practical joke. The next morning they (along with several Indians?) dressed in full Indian war costume, complete with tomahawks, blankets, and war paint. When Gage and Langdon began talking to the miller, a "large Indian" came from behind a tree and fired his rifle at the miller. Pretending to be shot, the miller fell to the ground, shouting, "My God, the Indians! I'm shot!" The other warriors yelled and swung their weapons. Gage ran to Lexington and Langdon to the

There was an old mill at Brighton, north of the intersection of State Road 120 and State Road 3 on the west side of the road. It is no longer standing, but a pond is nearby. Photo circa 1912; courtesy of Roberta May and J. Scott McKibben.

Right
Amos Long's store used to stand on State Road 120 near its intersection with State Road 3. It was a general store that sold Wells Mastiff shoes, among many other things. Courtesy of Roberta May.

Top right
Brighton's first car was built by Jacob Heign. Gifford Photo, 1910; J. Scott McKibben collection.

Bottom right
This is a Springfield Township School bus built by Jacob Heign of Brighton. Courtesy of Marian Deal.

western part of Greenfield Township, both warning each family they saw that all at the mill had been shot and the Indians were coming.

At Lexington, everyone gathered into George Donaldson's blacksmith shop. The men quickly cut down trees and built a fort. On the western side of the township, people constructed a fort on the island at Cedar Lake. Within a few days, the truth became known and the people went home. This incident became known as the Gage and Langdon War. Several people responsible for the fiasco were boycotted by townspeople and eventually left town.

Pretty Prairie received its name because it was pretty; English Prairie was named for its early residents from England. Knee-breeches and long stockings were worn by several of the Englishmen for years after their arrival.

In 1836 Elisha Shepard and Bazaleel Alvord platted a village on section 25, on the banks of Wall Lake, named Vistula. Unfortunately, it was just a "paper town."

John Kromer, surveyor, platted the village of Lexington in July 1836, on sections 25 and 30, for Abraham K. Brower and Joseph Skerritt. A post office was established there in the same year.

Forty years later, the name of the village was changed from Lexington to Brighton because of a confusion regarding post office names. Peter Beisel, who later owned Greenfield Mills, built a store building and opened a general store soon after Lexington was laid out. Other merchants were the Crandells and the Longs. Harvey C. Plank started an implement and hardware business at Brighton in 1905. In 1918 he added a grocery and general merchandise to his other business, which he continued for eight years. He was a Greenfield Township trustee for four years and later served as Clerk of the LaGrange Circuit Court (*LaGrange Centennial*).

The last named source also mentions talented and well-known residents of the area such as George Donaldson, a blacksmith who fashioned a native rock into a millstone; Isaac Lehmer, a sawmill operator and thresher who invented the first friction clutch traction threshing machine in the country and also built a gasoline-driven horseless carriage; Fleming Hopkins, a farmer who had the idea for the serrated sickle section used in McCormick grain harvesters; and Jacob Heign, a blacksmith and iron worker who built wagons, delivery trucks, motor school buses and passenger buses. Jane M. Clark was the first school teacher near Lexington. She taught sixty

BRIGHTON'S FIRST CAR.

BUILT BY JACOB HEIGN
BRIGHTON, INDIANA.

Cyrus Fillmore lived in this house on State Road 120 east of Brighton—almost to the Steuben County line. The house is now starting to fall down. A family cemetery was located nearby on 1000E and State Road 120. When 120 was widened, the cemetery was destroyed. According to Robert and Leonore Current in the *Cemeteries of LaGrange County Indiana,* there was still a stone in the old Fillmore house east of the cemetery site in the early 1980s. Many Fillmore tombstones are in the Brighton Chapel Cemetery, including one for Cyrus, who was born December 22, 1801, and died November 30, 1889. Courtesy of J. Scott McKibben.

pupils for two dollars per week. An abandoned log cabin southwest of town served as the first school.

Manufacturers began making all kinds of useful and needed objects such as furniture, axes, chisels, adzes, grubbing-hoes, brooms, spinning wheels, and shoes. Stores opened to sell the merchandise.

A famous religious revival took place at Pretty Prairie in 1840. A few years later, in 1843, the Congregation of Saints was organized at Lexington. Peter Long came to Greenfield Township in 1858. He was overseer of the English Prairie Church, which he helped found. He was also a preacher.

Other pioneers who contributed to the community were Joseph Pickles, John Whitlock, William D. Hall, Charles W. Stroud, Daniel Long, E. T. McCredie, Peter Alspaugh, Joseph Gunthorp, William and Mary (Millhuff) Horner, Christian J. Plank, and Adolph Sigrist.

Cyrus Fillmore came to Greenfield Township in 1837, lived on rented property for a few years, and then purchased 280 acres in 1843. His four children were Benjamin, Almon, Helen, and Millard C. In 1848 Cyrus's brother, Millard Fillmore of New York, was elected vice president of the United States. With the death of President Zachary Taylor, Millard Fillmore became president for nearly three years. Cyrus Fillmore was a trustee of Greenfield for twelve years. He was also a spiritualist, of which there were quite a few in the 1800s in LaGrange County.

A sawmill and gristmill were established in the northeastern corner of the township on Crooked Creek (Fawn River) in 1834 and 1846, respectively. Samuel Burnside erected the sawmill; Peter Bisel converted it to a gristmill. It was known as Davis' Mills, as was the village, after Amos Davis purchased the mill in 1854. He ran it until his death in 1867 at the age of seventy (*LaGrange, 1882*). The post office known as Greenfield Mills was established in 1875. A. E. Keagy served as postmaster at one time.

According to a brochure distributed by the Rinkel family regarding Greenfield Mills, Henry Rinkel, in 1904, traded a 240-acre farm and assumed the mortgage on the mill. Closed for six months due to the washing out of the dam, the mill was being used as a dance hall. The neighbors thought the mill was jinxed and questioned the wisdom of trying to reopen it. Nevertheless, they gathered together to help Henry rebuild the dam. As a result, he was able to move his family to Greenfield Mills the day after Thanksgiving, 1904.

It took a couple of years to get the mill in good running operation. When the dam washed out again, the neighbors helped Henry build another one—this time of concrete. Completed in 1908, this dam still holds back the water in the millpond. The mill has been in continuous operation since then.

Greenfield Mills now uses water-generated electricity to run its machinery rather than the original water power alone. Surplus electricity is sold to a few customers and to NIPSCO. Hydroelectric generators produce the power.

Henry Rinkel's son, George, moved back to Greenfield Mills in 1927 to help his father. When Henry died in 1945, George and his mother, Jennie Belle, kept the mill in operation. Howard Rinkel came home in 1949 to help his father, George. Howard and his wife, Helen Lee, have three sons, Hal, Dan, and David, and a daughter, Joyce. Mother Jennie Belle died in 1963.

George and Howard worked together to improve and expand their business. In 1973 they built a pneumatic mill that handles

The Greenfield Mills Store in 1908 was one block west of the mill. Later, George Rinkel operated a garage in it. His son, Howard, remembers the time someone ran a car through it and out the back wall. It is now a private residence. J. Scott McKibben collection.

everything by air. It has increased production rates. Howard's son, Dan, joined his father in 1975. George died in 1978 and his wife, Helen, in 1985. In 1988 Joyce began to help run the updated mill and also to lend a hand to her mother, Helen Lee, who does the bookkeeping. Joyce lives in the old store building.

The mill, with its three tall silos, appears fairly modern from the outside. It has had three additions. Inside, however, one can see part of the original floors and a lattice of handhewn beams. Five of the oak timbers are fifty feet long and ten inches square. Flour, pancake mix, and cereal are produced here in addition to electrical power. Known as Greenfield Mills, Inc., it is located on road 750N, northeast of Brighton and northwest of Orland. It is the only commercial water powered mill in the state.

On the corner across from Greenfield Mills is the former United Brethren Church. It belonged to the St. Joseph Valley Conference. Yoder photo, 1995.

Top left
At Greenfield Mills, this building used to be part of the large building with porches before that building became a store. Note the lightning rods on the roof. Yoder photo, 1995.

Bottom left
This house across the road from Greenfield Mills became a store after the first store became a garage. Porches and an addition were added to it after the original building was divided. Yoder photo, 1995.

Although it looks like a barn, and it was, this building was once the LaGrange County Courthouse, built of heavy hewn timbers on the square in LaGrange in 1843. It was moved in 1878 to what was later the Grubaugh farm on the first four corners east of Brighton (700E) on State Road 120, on the south side of the road. The original windows were removed, and it was resided several times. Owners tried to sell it for $500, but when there were no "takers," it was torn down in the early 1980s. Mike Fuller photo; courtesy of Mrs. Robert Simpson.

These barns (on 4160E State Road 120) between Brighton and Howe were on the farm of Fred and Clara (Anderson) Horning. The barns, a house, and windmill were pictured in the 1874 atlas and still remain today, all around 150 years old. Former owners were William Fish, Charles Shoup, William Anderson, the Hornings, William and Josephine Tjarks, and Wilbur and Esther Tjarks. Current owners are Richard and Lisa Tjarks, who live there with son Adam. They found a leather stencil of the name SHOUP in the wall during a recent residing. Research reveals that Lisa is the great-great-granddaughter of Calista (Shoup) and James Kline Sr. Calista was the sister of former owner, Charles Shoup. Courtesy of Richard and Lisa Tjarks.

The new Greenfield Township Consolidated School was erected in 1921; A. M. Strauss, Fort Wayne, architect; G. E. Miller & Son of Stroh, contractors. When Lakeland High School was built, Brighton high school students attended there, starting in 1965. In its last years as a public school, it was an elementary. Now elementary students attend Lima-Brighton Elementary in Howe. Maranatha Christian Fellowship has bought the building. Yoder photo, 1995.

Built as Greenfield Township Graded School, this was the first brick high school in Brighton. Courtesy of Richard Marks.

Someone sailing on Cedar Lake during July of 1955. Courtesy of Verne Schlemmer.

One or more of the Schlemmer brothers (Verne, Donald, and David) are wading in a county lake. Photo circa 1920s; Schlemmer collection.

This old barn near Brighton on State Road 3 once belonged to Clarence and then Ledger Damer. It is currently being demolished. Yoder photo, 1995.

The Wolcottville Star Band has gathered to play at the fair.
Photo circa 1912; J. Scott McKibben collection.

6

Johnson Township

Levi Wright came to the area later known as Johnson Township in 1834. The township was not organized until March 6, 1837. He found the area inhabited by wild animals. An Indian village was located on the west bank of Oliver Lake, populated by Potawatomi Indians and half-breeds of French and Indian descent.

Nelson Nichols, Peter Lampson, Daniel Martin, and John Adams helped Wright build his cabin. Adams entered land on the shores of present-day Adam's Lake. Levi Wright became an influential man and owner of three hundred acres. The area on the line between sections thirteen and fourteen soon became known as Wright's Corners (*LaGrange, 1882*).

Listed in the *LaGrange Centennial* are others who settled around 1835 and built homes: Samuel Benham, Peter Tillspaugh, George Walker, John Hughes, Jeremiah Bidwell, Robert Meeker, John Doty, and Robert Latta.

They were followed by Thomas Oliver, Philo Taylor, George Wolcott, Henry Nichols, Almon White, Hiram Gardner, John

Right

Rachel Kitchen (1833–1916) is pictured with her third husband, Warren Lovell (1826–1914), a Civil War veteran. She also was married to Schuyler Nelson and a Hemminger. Both died. Rachel and Schuyler Nelson had a son, George, who had a son, Don, who had two daughters, Irene (Mrs. Clark Babcock) and Josephene (Mrs. Everett Miller). Rachel lived in a log cabin on the Oliver Lake road. According to family tradition, she remembers the Indians at Oliver Lake who would come to her home when they heard the family was going to Fort Wayne and ask for staples to be bought. The Indians also traded vegetables with them. The trip took two days going, two days to shop, and two days to return. Rachel and Schuyler lived in a log cabin, later, on Hawpatch. When Rachel married Warren Lovell, they lived in LaGrange on Townline Road. Photo circa late 1800s; Irene Babcock collection.

This is Main Street in Woodruff circa 1912. Gifford Photo; J. Scott McKibben collection.

According to the inscription above the door, this is "JOHNSON TP. Dist. No. 5 1901." Woodruff School burned on February 4, 1912, and was replaced with a similar three-room brick structure. Gifford Photo; courtesy of Richard Marks.

Vaughn, Samuel Koon, Levi Wildman, Joseph Caswell, William Hardin, Nathan Sherman, Arron Hill, Thomas Higgins, William, Taylor, James Oliver, Joseph Head, and Mr. Kimble.

The infamous Tamarack House, five miles south of Woodruff, was built as a means of trading between the whites and Indians. The tavern was built of tamarack poles with which it was built. Burris and Hitchcock built a dam and sawmill just south of it in 1836. In 1844 a gristmill was built on the south side of the river. The tavern became a refuge later for outlaws, horse thieves, counterfeiters, and men and women of ill repute (*LaGrange Centennial*).

In the unpublished "History of Woodruff," by Riley L. Case, he states his belief that Wright's Corners became a place of importance at an early day because of: first, its location "on the Lima Road, second, the early appointment of a postmaster, one year after the first settler arrived, and third, the convergence of five roads that enter the corners."

Lima Road was significant because it followed the path used by Indians and explorers to portage between Lake Michigan by the St. Joseph River to the Maumee and Lake Erie. A few miles west of Kekionga (now Fort Wayne), travelers could paddle a boat or canoe on the Wabash River, then go to the Mississippi River, and on to the Gulf of Mexico.

Wright's Corners had a post office named Marcey (or Marcy), which opened in 1835. On May 6, 1880, during Allen Woodruff's second term as postmaster, the name was changed to Woodruff. The post office was closed July 5, 1905. In 1844, Woodruff's store had burned. Other store operators were Charles W. Vaughn, Levi Wildman, Adams, Crandall, and Strayer.

The first school in the township was a log house at Wright's Corners, circa 1836. Other schools replaced it. In 1912, twelve students attended Woodruff High School for three years of instruction. In 1914, the high school was transferred to Wolcottville. The grades remained in Woodruff until 1937. The school had been in operation for 101 years. Doris Schemerhorn Troxel and Mrs. Bernice Fisher were the last teachers.

St. Johns Lutheran Church was built one mile west of Woodruff in 1860 at a cost of $1,600. The Woodruff Evangelicals started meeting in the school house. The present church was built in 1870 by capenters James Billman and William Snyder. After a couple of mergers, the Evangelical Church became Woodruff Grove United Methodist Church. With the exception of a few older homes and the cemetery, this church is all that remains of historical Woodruff, but many descendants of its pioneers remain throughout the county.

Wolcottville was platted April 6, 1853, by Joseph and Elizabeth Keasey. By 1837, the Wolcottville Baptist Church was organized. It

On October 7, 1907, there was an explosion in the building behind Sander's Hardware in Wolcottville. According to J. Scott McKibben, someone was trying out a new gun and fired it into the building where explosives were being stored. The result could be heard by Ledger McKibben four miles away in Valentine. Gerald Fisher collection; courtesy of Richard Marks and J. Scott McKibben.

Frank P. Sanders & Sons owned this hardware store in Wolcottville. Gerald Fisher collection, courtesy of Richard Marks.

was actually constructed in 1843. The Wolcottville Methodist Church was organized in 1839.

The north branch of the Elkhart River passes through Wolcottville. One of the first settlers, Philo Taylor, came in February 1837. A year later, he built the first schoolhouse. Originally, he owned the water-power, but sold it to George Wolcott who came in June of 1837. Wolcott built a carding mill, a gristmill, a sawmill, and a distillery, which he operated at different periods. He opened the first store in 1839. In 1851 he founded the Wolcottville Seminary. Miss Susan Griggs came from Vermont in 1852 to take charge of it. Students could study cultural subjects such as ancient and modern languages, music, and painting. It closed when the free-school system was established (*LaGrange Centennial*).

Some people believe Wolcott's Mills is the original name for this town, while others say it is Wolcottville. Wolcott's Mills is listed in the *Report of the Adjutant General of the State of Indiana 1861–1865* as the place of residence for Corporal Ira McCollum, Corporal David S. Bass, Private A. W. Deffenbaugh, and Private Samuel P. Metz, all in the 88th Regiment, Indiana Volunteers. The name lives on because the title given to today's elementary school in Wolcottville is Wolcott Mills.

Wildman's Exchange Bank was started in 1872–1873. It was taken over later by the State Bank of Wolcottville. S. P. Sanders started a hardware business in 1870. Westler and Axel owned and operated a flouring mill (*Combined Atlases*).

The Pennsylvania and Wabash railroads both helped businesses to grow in Wolcottville. Henry L. Taylor built a grain elevator in 1871. A creamery burned, but was rebuilt. Frederick Eugene Dickinson manufactured brick and tile in a factory located north of Wolcottville. Mrs. Mary Alger owned and operated a hotel known as the Commercial House. It was headquarters for the engineers who worked with the construction of the Wabash Railroad. John C. Scheffler started a drug and grocery store in 1877. He was also appointed postmaster by President Harrison. He was a Civil War veteran who served in the First Indiana Heavy Artillery, Company "A." David A. Vaughn established a livery business in 1886. Andrew R. Yeager & Son (Edwin E.) owned a lumber mill that burned in 1888. After it was rebuilt, Andrew's brother, Samuel, joined the firm for a time. Then he entered the furniture business. The Wolcottville foundry was established in 1890. The *Wolcottville Globe* was established in 1891 by J. R. Leonard. Edwin G. Cook began the practice of law in Wolcottville in 1892 (*Combined Atlases*).

Left
The Commercial House was located next to the hardware in Wolcottville. Musicians on the porch are playing guitars. Photo 1891; J. Scott McKibben collection.

Right
Men are waiting near the Wabash Railroad station in Wolcottville. Photo circa 1915; J. Scott McKibben collection.

The Valentine School was built in 1883 and was closed in 1932. It is on the farm of J. Scott McKibben. Yoder photo, 1995.

Valentine is located south of LaGrange and north of Wolcottville on State Road 9. Much of the following information regarding this community was obtained from the unpublished article of J. Scott McKibben entitled "Valentine."

A log schoolhouse was erected circa 1840 and was used until 1843. Thomas Oliver furnished part of the lumber, and Abraham Eiman made the shingles. One of the builders, Hiram Gardner, provided a place to board for the teacher, Elmira Crandall, who paid him two bushels of corn per week for her board.

A mother, three children, and the dog are posed in front of their home in Valentine. They may be part of the Hart family. Photo circa 1908; Lela Stanner collection.

The original school was replaced by another log one on the Schoonover farm. It burned in 1857. A small frame building was built on ground purchased from James and Sarah McKibben for one hundred dollars. After it was closed and moved from the property, it reverted back to the McKibbens.

In 1883 James and Lissa McKibben deeded a different site to Johnson Township where a two-room brick school was built. It served the community until 1932 when the pupils were bused to Wolcottville.

The Grand Rapids and Indiana Railroad (later the Pennsylvania) reached Valentine in 1870–1871. Sargent and Clugston built a sawmill in 1870 that used steam double saws. In 1875 a large factory was built by Albert Scoville of Sturgis in which tool handles, staves, barrel headings, and butter-tubs were manufactured (*History of Northeast Indiana, Vol. I*).

William Painter was appointed the first postmaster in November 1873. Although the residents wanted to name the town Palestine, they were informed that this name already existed and that the name would be Valentine instead. No one knows why this name was chosen.

In 1874 William Painter opened an inn called Valentine House and added a general store in addition to the post office. Merchants who followed him were William Rowe, James D. Clugston, Oscar Gardner, Albert Markel, and Clark Betts.

James S. and Lissa A. McKibben platted the village of Valentine out of their farm in April 1879. Twenty-one lots were sold.

The Methodist Episcopal Church in Wolcottville is having a picnic on September 2, 1902. J. Scott McKibben collection.

Valentine had a lot of railroad activity. At one point there were three station operators. Eventually business lessened. In 1930 the station house was moved to Wolcottville, and the freight house became Sam Hart's woodshed.

A. M. Patton operated the black store built by his father, John Patton. He was the store operator and postmaster just before Ray VanDrew, who became postmaster in 1912. Mr. Sexton, Jim Vroman, Abe Raver, and John Rugg each operated it later. John Ward built a store on the lot where John Beach's store burned in 1891. Jason Calvert operated it before selling it to Ray VanDrew, who was in business until 1965.

The Valentine Inn was a large sprawling building with several wings. These wings were removed and relocated as private homes. Other houses were also moved from their original locations. Across from the black store, on the Sargent and Clugston mill lot, was the home of Bert Hart and his family.

George Slack was the first blacksmith. Others were Jim LaRue and Tom Oliver. According to McKibben, Oliver's shop was "a large two-story frame building with a hall over it where box socials, political rallies, etc., were held." It was torn down about 1915.

The Methodist Episcopal Church of Valentine was organized in 1876. James S. and Lissa A. McKibben gave land for the church building. It was constructed in 1880 and the parsonage in 1881. The McKibben's own brick house was built in 1882. It is now the home of J. Scott McKibben.

An advertising card from the Riverside Milling Company uses a pretty woman to sell their flour. J. Scott McKibben collection.

A postcard dated June 1910 has this picture with the following message: "One act in the butterfly drill—good on children's day." It is probably in Wolcottville. J. Scott McKibben collection.

A team of horses pulling a wagon across the bridge in Wolcottville while children, one carrying a dog, use the footbridge. Photo circa 1912; Gerald Fisher collection; courtesy of Richard Marks.

College Hill in Wolcottville is named for the seminary that used to be here. The Wolcottville School was built in 1898 after the previous one burned in 1897. Photo 1913; Gerald Fisher collection; courtesy of Richard Marks.

A postcard dated 1909 shows downtown Wolcottville. Gerald Fisher collection; courtesy of Richard Marks.

Mr. Eshelman built and lived in this stone house on State Road 9 in Wolcottville. It appears in many early pictures of the town before the street was paved. Yoder photo, 1995.

There was a victory parade down the main street of Wolcottville to celebrate the end of World War I. Gerald Fisher collection; courtesy of Richard Marks and J. Scott McKibben.

Guy Richardson lived in this stately house in Ontario located next to the former Cain's Lumber. Yoder photo, 1995.

7

Lima Township

Benjamin Blair settled one mile west of present-day Howe in 1828, three years before Lima Township was organized on May 14, 1832. Nathan Fowler, James Thurston, William Thrall, Jonathan Gardner, and their families came soon afterwards.

The Potawatomi Indians and white settlers were both attracted to the area because of its location between Pigeon and Fawn Rivers. The best way to travel and transport goods in those days was by water. Wildlife was plentiful along the rivers, as well. North and South Twin Lakes, Still Lake, and Cedar Lake (partly in Lima but mostly in Greenfield Township) also attracted settlers.

When the Indians lived in what is now Lima Township, their village was known as Mongoquinong (Indian squaw). It may have been located on the site where Riverside Cemetery was established later.

On October 22, 1834, the town of Mongoquinong was laid out by surveyor John Kromer on land owned by Moses and Ica Rice. These men donated eighty-four lots to the town if the county seat would be located there.

According to the *History of Northeast Indiana, Vol. I,* old Lima "had for centuries been an Indian village widely known." The Indians used to hoe their corn-hills on the present site of Howe School. In Marguerite E. Smith's "Early History of Howe," *A History of Lima Township, LaGrange County, Indiana,* she says that there were probably no more than thirty wigwams standing at Mongoquinong in 1828, scattered along the Pigeon River.

In 1834 Mongoquinong became known as Lima. A post office was established in what is now Springfield Township and the name Mongoquinong went along. Later, in 1909, the post office and the station on the Pennsylvania Railroad were both named Howe in honor of John B. Howe, so the town also took on his name. Another reason for the change is because mail and freight destined for Lima, Ohio, often were sent to Lima, Indiana, and vice versa.

As early as 1829, the Ica Rices sold the Indians whiskey, tobacco,

lead, and other supplies. Moses Rice had the first store. Outside the town limits, Thomas Gale and George Egnew each had a store. Arthur Burrows ran a tavern in 1833. Other merchants were Delavin Martin with a $12,000 stock and Gale & Williams, afterwards by Samuel P. Williams. The latter store, which opened in the spring of 1837, had goods valued at $25,000. According to the *History of Northeast Indiana, Vol. I,* these goods were "purchased in New York City and shipped via Erie Canal to Buffalo, transported by vessel to Michigan City, then hauled in wagons to Lima, the freight bill alone amounting to about $3,000."

Lima grew rapidly. In 1836 the Samuel P. Williams addition was added to the north. He donated a block for a public park or square. Norman Merriman opened a hotel in 1835. By 1840, there were 450 people living in town.

In 1836 Albert Powell built a distillery at "Still" Lake. Hiram Harding took over the business later. He was succeeded by H. Wood who removed the still and started a potash factory. A brick and tile kiln was built near Still Lake in later years that provided the brick to rebuild the block buildings east of the town square in the 1860s *(History of Lima).*

In 1852 the Lima Seminary for young ladies was founded by S. P. Williams in block 12 of the Williams' addition. It lasted for ten years.

The Kingsbury House was begun as a hotel by N. R. Kingsbury in 1863. C. D. Kingsbury took charge in 1890, followed by his

A frame courthouse was built on the public square of the original plot of Lima. A frame jail was built on the square's southwest corner. Professional people were attracted to the county seat with the good location on the rivers. One of these was the town's namesake, John B. Howe, the first teacher, lawyer, and banker and the founder of Howe School. In 1844, the town was disheartened by the removal of the county seat to the town of LaGrange. Citizens of Howe later bought the public square, seen in this picture, from the county commissioners and gave it to Lima Township as a town park. Carlie Deal collection; courtesy of Marian Deal.

Top left

Riverside Cemetery in Howe was established on the site of a Potawatomi Indian village. Yoder photo, 1995.

Bottom left

The Howe Military band standing at attention one day in 1936. Courtesy of Beverly Warner.

In 1887, the Lima Township Consolidated High School was the first in the state to be commissioned and the first in the county to receive a first class commission in 1923. This building was demolished. Only the bell tower stands on the grounds as a monument. The present school on this site is Lima-Brighton Elementary. Photo circa 1915; J. Scott McKibben collection.

William Hill built the brick business block at Lima in 1860–1861 and started a hardware store. Other owners in succession were: Sam Yeagla and brother Jacob; A. L. Yeagla and father Jacob; Arthur Atwater and Samuel Nichols; O. M. Warner and son David; David and Lynn Warner; David again; and Vernal Parish. Standing in Warner Hardware, left to right, are O. M. Warner, Lynn Warner, and Forrest Miller. Photo 1932; courtesy of Beverly Warner.

daughter, Fannie, and her husband, Clarence E. Schaeffer. In 1913, Mr. Schaeffer was appointed postmaster (*History of Lima).*

The Star Grist Mill on Fawn River was erected two miles northwest of Lima by Post and Torry. Later owners were George Fleisher, Mr. Ritzer, and O. P. McKee. Clyde and Mardell Wilson purchased the mill in 1981. They use it to generate electricity for their sixty-spot campground. Like Greenfield Mills, they sell electrical power to NIPSCO. In existence since 1857, they started generating electricity in 1929. In recent years, both mills have been in a struggle with the Federal Energy Regulatory Commission over their right to generate electricity. In July 1993, the LaGrange County Commissioners passed an ordinance stating that both mills are of historical significance and aid in controlling floods in the county.

According to the *History of Lima,* two of the newspapers published in Lima were the *Lima Democrat* (1845) and the *Lima Union* (1860–1863). Among the advertisements from the latter paper were: Oliver Lampman—Justice of Peace, Silversmith, one door east of railroad tracks on Ontario Road; Rawles & Hull, Dry goods, groceries, hardware, one door west of Lima Bank (want to buy $10,000 worth of fur); Thomas Howlett, Boots & Shoe Mfg., northeast corner of Third and Defiance Streets (where the fire station is located in 1995); Kendallville & Sturgis Hack Line; R. H. Morrison & William Hill, buyers of farms.

According to Glen E. Libey in the *History of Lima,* a windmill factory was started in 1885 at the site of present-day George Reid & Son well and plumbing business. It contained a woodworking department and a foundry. The organizers were George W. Libey and Charles Nichols. These windmills were known as the "Queen." In the 1880s, there was a town windmill and a large wooden tank on a tower at the northeast corner of the park. It supplied water to a horse tank and also water hydrants.

Farmers in the township raised mostly corn, wheat, hay, oats, and vegetables. Large quantities of potatoes and melons were shipped to distant markets by railroads, at first, and later also by trucks. Pickles were a cash crop for some farmers. According to the *History of Lima,* N. A. Parham ran a pickle station in 1921, south of the elevator. He shipped nine tons of pickles that year. Maurice Andrews was in charge of this station at a later date, as well as stations in Michigan.

Guy Richardson was one of the major melon growers in the Ontario-Howe area. A well-educated man, he was one of the first to use lime or marl to sweeten the soil. He developed different varieties of muskmelons. Some of these were: Honey Rock, Rocko Honey, and later Pride of Wisconsin and Queen's Best. These old varieties are either no longer available or hard to get.

Other local melon growers and/or shippers were Giles Long, Ed Wunder, Joe May, John Rush, and Howard Boyd. In the Mongo area were Smith, Haskins, and Weiss.

This area shipped melons all over the country by the semi-loads to Chicago, Toledo, and Cleveland markets. Diamond T trucks were used to transport melons by Ed Wunder. He and his wife, Effie, lived on Old 9 (100E), between Howe and LaGrange, and across the road from Joe May. Wunder had a machine that sorted according

Watermelons were grown in many varieties. Cannon Balls, Southern Greys, and Keckley Sweets were area favorites. Big watermelons sold for fifty cents each during the 1930s. Shown enjoying the melons are Bloomfield Township farmer Floyd Connelly (center) and his son, Arnold (left), who have grown their share of melons over the years, and their neighbor, Frank Aldrich. Photo circa 1935; Connelly collection.

to size. Blemished or cracked melons were rejected. Three different sizes of muskmelons were crated and stored in his packing shed, awaiting shipment.

Some of the growers, such as Joe May and John Rush, sold locally from their farms. John Rush also lived on Old 9 (100E).

The village of Ontario was platted on May 30, 1837, in the southwest quarter of section 33 by Nathan Jenks, a native of Ontario County, New York. Prior to the platting, in February of the same year, a meeting was held in Lima to establish a Christian literary institution to be known as the LaGrange Collegiate Institute. It was to be patterned after Oberlin College in Ohio. According to John W. Hanan in the *LaGrange Centennial,* a decision was made to locate it in the village of Ontario. (It was actually built just over the line in Bloomfield Township.) Nathan Jenks was the principle founder of the institution.

A Presbyterian Church was organized in Ontario in 1840. The Methodists organized a church in 1869 and erected it a bit later. This church, located by the town square, burned in 1939; it was not replaced.

In 1842 a newspaper, the *LaGrange Freeman,* was started in Ontario by Samuel Hemingway. It was followed, in 1844, by the *People's Advocate.*

George Latterer settled on the site of Ontario in 1834. So did

Left page bottom
Building began on the LaGrange Collegiate Institute in 1837. School was taught in 1838–1839 by Mr. and Mrs. Cyrill W. Wilson using the buildings which were still unfinished. They also ran a boarding house. Soon fifty students enrolled. The two and one-half story educational building was completed along with a barn, workshop, etc. A Congregational Church was erected on the grounds as well. Although the school was closed occasionally due to sickness and war, the institution's 1872 catalog lists 1,471 different students as alumni. Rufus Patch was one of the well-known principals. Free high schools and preparatory schools caused the college to close in 1879. The building was destroyed by the Palm Sunday tornado in 1965. J. Scott McKibben collection.

Left above
James Scott, an English weaver, came to Ontario in 1857 where he began work in the woolen mill. During the Civil War, the mill ran night and day to keep up with the demand. James Scott's son, Joseph G., bought the mill in 1874. Scott Woolen Mills, shown here, was a successful operation until 1886–1887 when the larger mills began to affect its trade. Mr. Scott was elected county treasurer in 1888 and the mill was sold in 1891. It eventually closed. J. Scott McKibben collection.

Right above
This is the Willard gristmill in Ontario. J. Scott McKibben collection.

The Carney-Frost Funeral Home formerly belonged to Lima merchant A. W. Beecher. It was built in the Italianate style and once had a rooftop cupola. It is located at 501 Defiance Street (or U.S. 120) in Howe. Once the Shoup Funeral Home, it was purchased in 1980 by the Carney-Frost Funeral Home and became the Shoup-Carney-Frost Funeral Home. Yoder photo, 1995.

This antique sideboard was made in Lima (Howe) at the Matchett shop. Courtesy of Marian Deal.

This antique desk was originally a table made by Doolittle at Ontario. Courtesy of Marian Deal.

Part of the Locust Lane Jersey Farms is designated as a Century Farm (100 years of ownership by the same family). It is now the home of Richard Kelly, son of Ralph Kelly, founder of Locust Lane Jersey Farms. This house on State Road 120 was built circa 1850s. Yoder photo, 1995.

Following page

Circa 1870, this fine home was built in section 20 by Butler Peter and Mary (Crawford) Gilbert, Ohio natives, who settled in Lima Township. Later, their eldest son, Allen, lived there with his family. Allan and Sarah (Collar) Gilbert are the couple in the buggy. Their twin sons, Allen Butler Gilbert (left) and Elvie Crawford Gilbert (right), standing with the dog, were born July 17, 1892. Mr. Butler's brothers, John and Niles, are probably the men on bicycles. The house changed hands and stood empty for over forty years before it was torn down. Photo circa 1897; courtesy of George Gilbert.

Alvin (Bill) Luginbill was employed at Locust Lane Jersey Farms run by Ralph A. Kelly. Margarete (Doll) Kelly photo, circa 1929; courtesy of Richard Kelly.

James Kline, LaGrange County's first County Extension Agent, is shown here with his prize-winning corn which was awarded a sweepstakes at the 1911 State Corn Show. Gifford Studio; courtesy of Katherine Swartzentruber.

Members of the Jersey Calf Club are lined up in the street at Howe to show off their calves. The club was organized in 1925 by County Agent James Kline. Ralph Kelly was an adviser. The State Bank of Lima financed the club. The Lima Creamery Company and the National Jersey Cattle Club were also sponsors. Photo circa 1929; courtesy of Katherine Swartzentruber.

Pioneers John and Marie Elizabeth (Engkler) Keefus, who were born in Germany, but met in Erie, Pennsylvania, and married on April 4, 1857, lived on the shore of South Twin Lake. They lived first in a log house and then built the brick house in the background of this picture in 1872. Great-great-grandson Peter Roger Kamphues and his family now own and occupy the house. John (1830–1926) and Elizabeth (1838–1928) are seated in front of their house. Courtesy of Katherine Swartzentruber.

Following page
An iron bridge, no longer in use, spans Pigeon River near Pigeon Lake, west of Howe. Yoder photo, 1995.

North Twin Lake was the site of a picnic held July 4, 1937. Among those attending were Mary Clark and her great-granddaughter, Mary Ann Babcock. Irene Babcock collection.

The Twin Lakes were always a favorite summer gathering place for the Kline cousins, family of James and Katherine (daughter of John and Elizabeth Keefus) Kline. At North Twin Lake are Erma Crampton (seated left), Florence Kline (seated right), and Eva (Kline) Swartzentruber (far right). Courtesy of Katherine Swartzentruber.

A bandstand can be seen in the town square of Ontario. The Congregational Church is to the right. Courtesy of Katherine Swartzentruber.

The Congregational Church in Ontario was dedicated in 1854 and has been a Congregational Church during most of that time. Different denominations have occupied it in recent years. Yoder photo, 1995.

Hallie Schindler operated the Ontario Store, which sold everything from ice cream and cookies to overalls, work shoes, and fly spray in hand pumps. On November 1, 1901, he moved the post office here where he served as postmaster for thirty-four years until 1943. Later, he sold the store to Gail Combs. Emery Straub was the last owner and ran the store for many years. It closed in 1980. On May 27, 1995, the building was sold at auction to Steve Mickem who is planning to open it again. Photo circa 1970; J. Scott McKibben collection.

These children are in front of Ontario School. The two-story building is now an apartment house. Photo circa 1903; J. Scott McKibben collection.

The "Laboratory" at the cement plant was home to the Emil Stroh family when they came to visit. It has been well maintained and is now a private residence. Yoder photo, 1995.

The Wabash Portland Cement Company stood on the shore of Big Turkey Lake. Photo circa 1930s. Richard Kelly collection.

The actual layout of Stroh was platted by Calvin Van Auken. He included town lots and locations for the cement plant, stockyards, elevator, and the railroad depot. He also engineered the building of the factory and laboratory with living quarters in the upper two stories. A spur of the Wabash Railroad was built from Helmer to the plant.

The plant operated around the clock with two twelve-hour shifts. It provided work for many people in both towns and the surrounding area from the time it opened in 1900 until it closed in 1941.

Some of the early settlers were Jacob Reed, Mrs. Dora Clinesmith who had a hotel, Perkins, Lowers, Wesley Hyer, John Deal, Alonzo

Bower, E. and A. Reinhart, William Shedley, and Roy Ford, who ran a general store from 1901 to 1920. William Hayward had a grain elevator and flour mill. Henry Rinkel was the miller. Other merchants were P. K. David, Harvey Hall, Walter Baden, Fred Schneider, Homer Smith, John Allen, J. C. Allen, Clyde Miller, A. A. Smith, Roy Turner, Willis Appleman, and Henry Lieberenz. The post office was established in 1900 with William Hayward as postmaster.

Elmira is located near the western shores of Big Turkey Lake. According to Marguerite Forst, a new road was built between the

Cement plant stockholders are Emil Stroh (left), the Duffield brothers (light suits in middle), and Mr. Stevens (far right). McKibben collection.

Below
These factory workers are thought to be from the cement plant. Photo circa 1930s; Rex Fisher collection.

According to Bertha (Perkins) Noll, this stately home in Elmira was once the home of Harriet (Perkins) Miller. Yoder photo, 1995.

Turkey Lake Restaurant and Tavern faces Big Turkey Lake in Elmira. Yoder photo, 1995.

properties of Jacob Forst and Jacob Perkins, which joined another road coming in from the west a mile away. Perkins' lots were to the south and Forst's to the north. Some of the people who owned homes on Forst's lots were Godfrey Lieberenz, L. L. Johnson, John Palmer, Elmer Forbes, Ed Erwin, and Newton Keyes. Mike Coney had a blacksmith shop, Lucius Harter a saloon and pool room, and Jacob Forst and Byron Greenman had a meat market which George Tritch eventually turned into a grocery. Business places and homes also were built on Jacob Perkins' lots.

At the north end of Main Street was a livery barn. Will Pray and later Jacob Dunbar ran a grocery store. Mr. Kenney owned a saloon. George Keesler built and operated a hardware store but sold it later to Will Lieberenz. Mrs. Lieberenz had a millinery shop in one end of the store. James Spearow built a hotel.

Jacob Perkins' house was built on the main street on the corner where the road turns east to go to Stroh. Isaac Perkins was in the lumber business. He had a large cement block house and a lumber shed with a barn and office in one end. The Perkins brothers owned several houses.

A newspaper, the *Stroh Times*, was published at the beginning of the century by Myers Brothers Publishers, Chris R. Myers, editor. It was a successor to the *South Milford Help*. Subscriptions cost one dollar per year if paid in advance.

The issue on September 19, 1901, tells a great deal about the new town. For example:

There is a large ad for The Stroh Roller Mill and Elevator; William Hayward, proprietor, and R. J. Willard, miller. They pay cash for grain and have flour for sale or exchange.

C. F. Cole has an ad for a harness and shoe shop in Stroh. He also promises to have a large line of buggies in a few days.

R. C. Lyman of Stroh had lots for sale in town. He says that Stroh came into existence on October 15, 1899, at 10 AM, when there was nothing there but wilderness and an "old leaning straw shed." In just under two years, the town has seventy-five good buildings and over three hundred inhabitants. Lyman encourages potential buyers by saying, "Do you wish to become rich? Never will such an opportunity present itself again."

Walker's Market in South Milford has for sale fresh and salt meats, fruits and canned goods; the market buys produce, poultry, and hides. Will Walker has just sold the market to G. W. Cochran.

Monday, September 16, 1901, school started with sixty-two pupils. Miss Nettie Ashley and George R. Leonard were the teachers.

J. H. Turner, proprietor of Stroh Livery and Feed Barn, which rents rigs by the hour or day. C. W. Dancer, M.D. has an office in E. Fiandt's store in Stroh. Jacob Reed owns The Reed Restaurant where meals cost twenty-five cents. Board is $1.00 per day or $3.15 per week. The barber, Rial Bell, of Stroh, advertises himself as a tonsorial artist. The upcoming Kendallville fair, September 30–October 4, 1901, would feature the Melrose aerial high-wire bicycle attraction. Thus ends the newspaper account.

On June 15, 1915, Stroh Farmers State Bank was organized with Harvey Lewis acting as chairman. There were forty stockholders. Harvey B. Lewis was elected president and Jacob Forst vice president. Directors were Sam Stout, Eugene Goodsell, Ralph R. Ousterhout, A. E. Emerson, Roscoe Conklin, Minor S. Perkins, and J. B. Hayward. Emil Stroh, president of the Wabash Portland Cement Company of Detroit, served on the board during 1917 and 1918.

The bank presidents have been Harvey B. Lewis (1915–1922), Samuel Stout (1923–March 1928), Jada Perkins (March 1928–September 1928), Minor S. Perkins (September 1928–1940), Floyd A. Perkins (1941–1975), and Miles S. Perkins (1976–continuing to the date of this writing).

Minor S. Perkins was on the first Board of Directors. Later he followed his brother, Jada, as president. Floyd followed his father, Minor, and Miles S. followed his father, Floyd, as president.

The Perkins family has been prominent in the Stroh/Elmira area for many years. Jacob Perkins, a Pennsylvania native of German descent, and his wife, Sarah A. Phipps, an Ohio native of English descent, came to Milford Township with baby Samuel in arms. Samuel had been born in Pennsylvania on August 21, 1834. They came with Jacob's mother and his two brothers, Enoch and Samuel. Jacob entered land from the government and built a double log house for his growing family. Other children were Elizabeth, Mary (Mrs. William Dunbar), Jacob, twins (born and died in 1841), Jerimiah (who married Fanny High), Harriet (Mrs. Nelson Miller), Sarah Jane (Susan on her tombstone, Mrs. John Forst), Dianna (1849–1851), Amanda (Mrs. William Day), and Isaac (who married Jennie Frederick). According to Maude (Perkins) Murray, Jacob, her grandfather, was killed in 1862 at the Wert sawmill when a pile of logs rolled over him.

Jacob's brother, Samuel, died at age thirty-one. He never married. His other brother, Enoch I, and his wife, Adaline, had five children:

Stroh School was built in 1902. It had eleven grades through 1929 and eight grades through 1957. It was demolished and the site became a town park. Photo circa 1915; Rex Fisher collection.

The Wabash depot in Stroh in 1911. The tracks were removed in 1945. McKibben collection.

Stewart, Job, Enoch II, Sarah Mariah, and Elizabeth. The sons were all Civil War veterans. His mother lived to be seventy-eight.

Samuel Perkins and his wife, Sarah Emma, daughter of Hugh W. and Margaret Ann (Appleman) Mains, had five sons: Jada, Miles Ellis (who died at age two), Minor S., Clyde, and Roy. Their first two children were born in Noble County where they lived for six years. The others were born in LaGrange County. Samuel's brother, Jacob (Jake), a founder of Elmira, was a single man. Isaac (Ike), the lumberman, was in business with Edward Miller. Ike was the father of Maude (Mrs. Max Murray), who served on the Board of Directors of Farmers State Bank for fifteen years until a tragic car accident claimed her life and that of her husband. According to Samuel's granddaughter, Bertha (Perkins) Noll, he was injured by a log rolling on his leg while cutting timber. He had gangrene in his leg and died on April 12, 1881, just five months before Roy was born. Before he died, he wrote a letter to each of his children, including the unborn baby. Mrs. Noll still has his letter to Minor which follows:

Saturday, March 26th, 1881

Miner my heart bleeds, to die and leave you on the cold world. I want you to try to be good to one another and not quarrel. Stick together like brothers and above all things be good to your mother. I want you to try to be truthful in all your dealings and try to do right—as near as your judgement will teach you. I want you to learn to be saving and put your money to a good use. These are the dying requests of your father. Please keep them.

—Samuel Perkins

Mrs. Perkins, who lived until 1906, had to raise the family alone.

Her four sons became successful farmers and owners of the Stroh Grain Company. They also engaged in drainage contracting. All four became involved in Farmers State Bank.

Stroh farmers are working in the onion fields. Onions were shipped on the Wabash Railroad to distant markets. Photo circa 1930; McKibben collection.

Big Turkey Lake was the site of an ice harvesting business. The railroad shipped ice and cement at the same time—when Stroh was new. McKibben collection.

Stroh Farm Supply, Inc., is a vital part of the farming community. Yoder photo, 1995.

Lake Bethel Church of God and cemetery are located on the south side of 250S at 1050E. Yoder photo, 1995.

A house caught fire north of Mt. Pisgah Store and the fire department arrived to fight it. Schlemmer collection.

Civil War veterans had a yearly reunion at Lakeside Park, half a mile from Mt. Pisgah, and at Smith's Grove in Mongo. The gatherings were well attended. Robert Yoder's ribbon collection; Yoder photo.

Before the advent of water amusement parks, swimmers slid down the slide into Pretty Lake. Photo circa 1950s; Connelly collection.

The railroad overpass in South Milford was completely rebuilt in 1993. Originally there was an old wooden overhead bridge. The Wasbash Railroad replaced it in 1923 with a concrete viaduct. Yoder photo, 1995.

Right page
South Milford area farmers depend on South Milford Grain, Inc., to supply their feed and buy their grain. Yoder photo, 1995.

One of the oldest homes in South Milford is on the west side of State Road 3. Yoder photo, 1995.

The Lakeshore and Michigan Southern Railroad passed through Shipshewana in 1888. The Valley Line arrived in 1905. Where the trains are in this picture, there is now a parking lot, and the depot (the first building in town, built in 1888) is the Galarina Folk Arts. Photo 1954; McKibben collection.

9

Newbury Township

This township received the name Newbury to distinguish it from its neighbor to the west, Middlebury. It was surveyed in 1830 and organized in 1837. Some of the first settlers were: Almon Lawrence, Alexander Poynter, Joseph Keasey, Amos Davis, Franklin Goodnow, Shrake, Styles, Patrick Nelson (a weaver born in Ireland) and family, Willard Cotton and family, George and Millicent Winter, John and Peter Keightly, Hornby, Truman Wilkinson, Esick Green, George Hilt, Berry, Obadiah Lawrence, Peter Schermerhorn, and Woodbridge.

The first election was held at Truman Wilkinson's place in section 17 on April 3, 1837. Thirteen people were eligible to vote. Of course women were not included in this early day. Those elected were Amos Davis, Justice of the Peace; Willard Cotton, Constable; Elijah West, Overseer of Poor; Franklin Goodnow and George Hilt, Road Viewers (*Combined Atlases*).

The first church was organized at the home of Joseph Nelson, son of Patrick, in the fall of 1837 by a Methodist evangelist, Rev. Brown. It started with nine members. Joseph Nelson was the class leader (*LaGrange, 1882*).

George Lotterer, who owned the site of Ontario in an early day, laid out a village called "Georgetown" on the shores of Shipshewana Lake in February 1837. It was never more than a "paper town" (*LaGrange, 1882*).

The first frame building in the township was a sawmill built on section 3 by West and Andrews in 1833. They also built a dam on Shipshewana Creek. Amos Davis built a sawmill on the Little Elkhart River, section 19, in 1838. Franklin Goodnow erected a frame barn on section 7. In 1837, Davis had hauled flour and other goods from Michigan City to Lima with five yokes of oxen (*Combined Atlases*).

Newbury Township, along with the rest of the county, suffered from the "ague and bilious fever" during 1838. A rainy spring and drought in the fall added to the misery.

Pashan Post Office was established in 1844 at the Amos Davis house. When he moved, it was closed. It was re-established in 1872 near the center of the township. Pashan School, Twp. No. 5, was built in section 21 on John Jones' land. In 1881 Harmon Stutsman owned a store there and served as deputy postmaster. Dr. Myers, the resident physician, served as postmaster. There was also a blacksmith shop (*LaGrange, 1882*).

Amos Davis was chosen as an associate judge for the county in 1839. He later served in the legislature, representing LaGrange and Elkhart counties in 1862–1864. He surveyed roads, helped found the Presbyterian Church, and operated Greenfield Mills. His wife, Susannah (Lieb), outlived her husband who died due to a fall. He was on his way to Bronson, Michigan, when he fell from a load of wheat, hitting his head on the wheel (*LaGrange, 1882*).

The town of Lake Shore was established on the shore of Hood's Lake (now Rainbow Lake), named for early settler Samuel Hood. In 1881 Dr. W. H. Shrock was appointed postmaster of the new post office named Shore. Twelve families lived there. Benedict Miller and Jacob Lupold had blacksmith shops. Shore School, Twp. No. 6, was built on Jacob Wiler's land in section 14. The Mennonites erected a church in the fall of 1874 on the shore of the lake. Amos Walters owned a steam-sawmill built in 1870 by Charles and Monroe Atwater and did a big business in lumber (*LaGrange, 1882*).

According to George Curtis in *A Patchwork Sampler,* Shore, as the town became known, had two stores. The merchants were John Kauffman and Jake Eash. In December 1883, the general store blew

The Shore Mennonite Church stands on land donated by William Wiler. The original location was across the road on the shore of Rainbow Lake. The church pictured here was built in 1965 after the Palm Sunday tornado destroyed the previous one. Yoder photo, 1995.

The Davis Hotel, built in 1890, had the brick removed before it was moved to its present location in November 1960. Courtesy of Margaret Simpson.

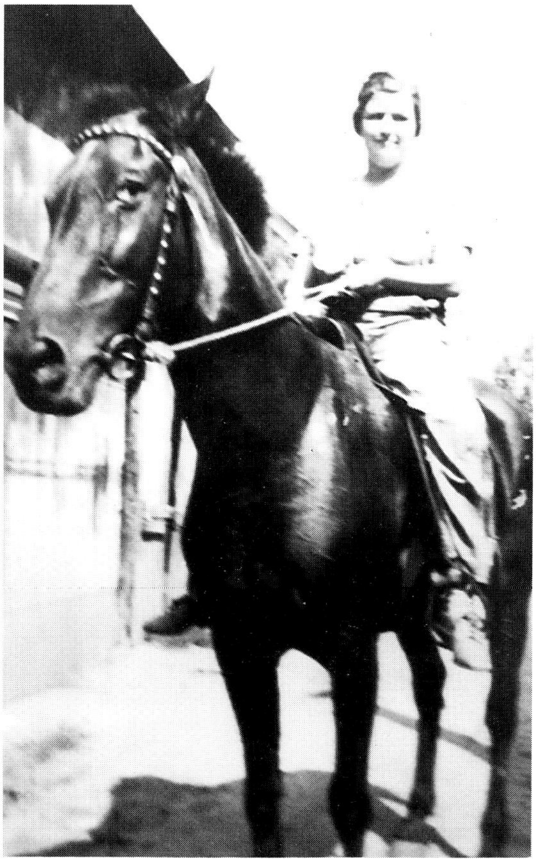

Sarah Davis, granddaughter of Hezekiah Davis and daughter of Hewlitt, was born in Shipshewana in 1912. She was a nurse. Photo circa 1930s; courtesy of Margaret Simpson.

up and burned due to a powder explosion. A few years later, when the railroad passed through the area to be known as Shipshewana, the village lost business and residents to the new town.

In the southeast corner of the township is the town and post office of Emma, formerly Eden Mills. The sawmill there was within Newbury Township and owned by Joseph Schrock. Jacob and Andrew Hostetler owned the Emma Store. Jacob was postmaster (*LaGrange, 1882*).

Hezekiah Davis, son of Amos and Susannah, grew up in the Pashan area of Newbury Township and married Sarah R. Reynolds. He worked hard and saved enough money to buy 1,400 acres of land. When the brick LaGrange courthouse was built, he was county commissioner. He founded the town of Shipshewana, laying out the first plat in January 1889. The Lakeshore and Michigan Railroad passed through the north part of town. This line from Goshen to Battle Creek was called the "Pumpkin Vine," named for its angling path. The first train went through the Shipshewana area in 1888.

Davis built a three-story business block and the Davis Hotel. Both of these still stand although the hotel has been moved. Hostetler's Drug Store is in the business block today with Davis Hall above it. According to Maurice Davis in *A Patchwork Sampler,* the public hall was known for the chautauquas where a noted speaker would appear, societies would debate, and plays would be performed.

Shipshewana was built near an old village once inhabited by the Potawatomi Indians who were forced to march to Kansas from September 4 to November 4, 1838. The government removed 867 Indians from Indiana. Twenty-seven children and eleven adults died on the way. Chief Shipshewana was allowed to return to Shipshewana Lake where he died two years later. A monument was erected to his memory on May 30, 1931. His descendant, John Shipshee, became a Deputy U.S. Marshal and veteran of the Civil according to a set pattern. There are regional variations of style. Females do not cut their hair. It is pinned up and kept covered with prayer caps and bonnets in public. Men and boys have blunt haircuts covered by a hat—black wool felt or straw. Married men have beards but no mustaches.

Amish speak their own version of the Deutsch language and use German Bibles, although they also speak English to outsiders and use English in school. Mennonites speak English, although some of them understand Deutsch.

Amish homes do not have electricity or telephones. Most sects do not allow cars; transportation is by horse and buggy. Mennonites do not have these restrictions.

Religion, family, and farming are the main concerns of the Amish in LaGrange County. Some, however, work in factories or businesses when farm income has dwindled or land has become scarce or expensive.

Mennonites have far-reaching concerns. The Mennonite Board of Missions oversees projects in foreign countries as well as at home. Young people often spend up to a year in foreign or domestic service, helping those less fortunate and serving as a witness of faith. Many local Mennonites receive higher education at Goshen College in adjoining Elkhart County.

James Mishler had a steam-powered threshing rig. Rena Markley collection.

Farver Lumber Company began in Shipshewana in 1889 when Jonathan and William Farver moved to town from south of Rainbow Lake. Their father, Abraham, owned the Klondike sawmill nearby. Jonathan built Hezekiah Davis' red brick buildings. Farver Lumber has the same location today. Pre-World War I photo; Rena Markley collection.

Peerless Roller Mills was the first elevator east of Farvers Lumber in Shipshewana. Photo circa 1901; Simpson collection.

Shipshewana School was built in 1893. The girl in the dark coat with arms raised (center) is Rena Nelson. Gifford Photo, circa 1911; courtesy of Rena (Nelson) Markley and Margaret Simpson.

A man and woman riding through a local lumberyard in a homemade car which, according to Rena Markley, was made and owned by a Mr. Reed about 1911. Simpson collection.

Men from William's South Mill are cutting wood in Shipshewana. Photo circa 1901; Simpson collection.

Sam Nelson (1876–1917) became a mail carrier in 1905 and used this open carriage and two western ponies to carry mail. The barn, on the corner of Middlebury and Harrison streets, later became Harry Yoder's garage. Sam died when he slipped on new straw in the haymow at John Bollinger's while threshing and fell, hitting his head. Courtesy of his daughter, Rena (Nelson) Markley.

This is Joe Hostetler's grocery wagon. Simpson collection.

BPB.B
1916

10

Springfield Township

Springfield Township was a part of Greenfield Township until May 1834 when a petition for organization was recognized. The petitioners were: John B. Clark, Jesse Huntsman, Joseph and Benjamin Foos, William C. Burn, Benjamin Jones, and William S. Prentiss. The first election held in the township was at the home of Benjamin Jones in August 1834 (*History of Northeast Indiana, Vol. I*).

In 1832 John B. Clark and Benjamin Jones bought the first two farms ever owned by white men in the area of Union Mills (later Mongo). At the same time, Mr. Brownell bought the water power at the union of Pigeon River and Turkey Creek whereby the name Union Mills originated. He had already constructed a gristmill there. At the same place in 1832, George Bulmer built the first sawmill. Two others were constructed later along Turkey Creek in sections 17 and 34. A wool-carding mill was established in 1835 (*Combined Atlases*).

Some of those who settled Springfield Township in an early day were George Thompson, Elijah Fothergill, Otis Shepardson, George Ray, William Bullmer, Samual Bradford, Norman Dyer, Jacob and Isaac Gage, David Michael, and Barnabas Thompson. Others who came before 1839 were Leonard Appleman, Russell Brown, Almon Brine, Isaac Carpenter, Moses Chapin, Conrad Deal, W. B. Dunn, George Donaldson, Edwin Davis, Robert Dayton, Rufus Freeman, John Hall, Luke Hammond, Charles Hull, Jehu Lackey, Job Gifford, and Richard Rice. In addition, there were Elisha Talmage, B. B. Waterhouse, Edward Smith, Harvey and Elisha Olmstead, and Samuel H. Wright (*History of Northeast Indiana, Vol. I*).

The village of Mongo was platted on sections 5 and 8 by Drusus Nichols in 1840. He bought Brownell's mill and operated it for many years. Later it was sold, along with a distillery and store. William Hall and Albert Powell were hotelkeepers. A whiskey keg factory was established in conjunction with the distillery. Erastus Haskins was a blacksmith. The first storekeeper was John O'Ferrell, a

Left page
The Brushy Prairie girls and boys had just enough players in 1916 to make up two teams. The girls' coach was Edna Greenawalt. Dorothy Harris collection.

The top view of Mongo on the bridge looking north shows the old store and hotel on the right. The bottom view shows someone crossing the Pigeon River bridge. Photo by V. W. Tryon, Kendallville; Marian Deal collection.

In March 1891, the Lodge of the Knights of Pythias was organized at Mongo. Dr. Albert B. Grubb gave land for the Knights of Pythias Hall shown here. Courtesy of Mary McCormick.

perpetrator of the "Gage and Langdon War." He may have been the first postmaster in 1833. Others believe it to have been Ephraim Seely, postmaster at Mongoquinong (Lima), who later moved to Springfield Township on section 4, taking the post office and name with him. Then, when Drusus Nichols bought the mill and built a store, he became the postmaster, acquiring the Mongoquinong Post Office's name. In 1873 the name was shortened to Mongo (*Combined Atlases*).

Leonard Appleman platted the village of Springfield in 1842 in sections 21 and 22. Lots were surveyed and 133 were offered for sale. During the 1840s, Brushy Prairie Post Office was established with Leonard Appleman as postmaster. It closed for a time during the Civil War and then reopened. Dr. A. M. Spaulding was postmaster for a long time. The post office closed in 1907. In later years, the village was called Applemanburg or Brushy Prairie.

The first school was built of logs on section 20 in 1835. Otis Shepardson was the teacher. Helen Wheeler taught in a second log school near J. B. Clark's home between sections 27 and 28. In 1839–1940, Russell Brown taught; eighty or more pupils attended. There was another log school at Talmage Corners. A combination church-school with a steeple on one end was built in 1855 in Springfield village. It was open until 1900 (*LaGrange Centennial*).

Leonard Appleman built a general store and warehouse, bought grain, and operated a pork packing business. Others opened businesses but, according to the *History of Northeast Indiana, Vol. I,* many of the early dealers were ruined by liquor. A temperance society was organized to combat the problem.

The Brushy Prairie Methodist Episcopal Society was organized by Rev. Thomas Birch Connelly in 1836. It started with a membership of eleven. A church was finally built in 1842 when Benjamin B. Waterhouse and others broke away from the Methodist society at Mud Corners in Milford Township and funded the building of Brushy Chapel in the southwest corner of section 33. It was the site of abolitionist meetings later. J. Lackey and others built the Springfield Methodist Church on section 26 in 1848. Baptist, Presbyterians, and United Brethren also held services but had no church buildings.

A communal living experiment took place in the township based on ideas of the socialist, Charles Fourier, whose philosophy was to organize people into self-sufficient cooperative communities. Everyone was supposed to share the work and receive equal pay. Possessions were pooled and land was acquired, beginning on the

The big building (left) was the old Brushy Prairie general store before it got moved around the corner on the left to U.S. 20. It was run by Lloyd Bassett, then Arnold, then Dewitt, then Teagarden, and then closed. Dorothy Harris collection.

Brushy Prairie Hall stood beyond the general store before the store was moved. It was the site for school Christmas programs and potluck dinners on the last day of school. Mary McCormick collection.

The former Mongo State Bank (1915–1926) is better known today as "Sarge's Tavern," alluding to the late Wesley Frye who ran a tavern there for many years. Yoder photo, 1995.

Mongo High School was built in 1912 at the north edge of Mongo where State Road 3 takes a sharp turn. It replaced the two-story frame structure. When the schools were consolidated, the high school was closed. It was demolished a few years ago. Photo circa 1920s; Marian Deal collection.

brick store buildings were also built. Mongo State Bank was built in 1915, but closed in 1926. The Moorish Floor Tile Company was established, but it went out of business after the railroad stopped operating. Some of its tile can still be seen in the floor at the former hospital (*LaGrange Centennial*).

A terrible storm, one of the worst in history, struck Springfield Township and townships to the west on the night of June 27, 1929. Numerous large trees and several barns were blown down. No one was injured or killed. The tornado followed the route of U.S. 20 from west of LaGrange and through town, through Plato, and on into Springfield Township. Orchards and windmills were damaged.

The Rollin Spearow farm had two barns wrecked and the roof and other parts of the house badly damaged in the 1929 tornado. Elster Photo; Rex Fisher collection.

The old hotel in Mongo has served people in many ways. From 1955 to 1959, it was Marks' Nursing Home run by Marie Marks. It has also held an ice cream shop, a restaurant, The Field and Stream Gallery, and a store that sold Mexican food. It is presently closed. Yoder photo, 1995.

Noah and Mahetable Brown Hall and an unidentified woman are in front of their Springfield Township home. This place is now the home of Bob Martin. J. H. Bowman Photo, Fort Wayne; Mary McCormick collection.

Right page
Hilda Wallace Hughes, graduate of LaGrange High School, class of 1907, is in her room at Northwestern University where she earned a bachelor's degree in 1915. Hilda Hughes collection; courtesy of Rex Fisher.

Ernest Talmage, driving his Farm-All tractor and pulling a combine. Mary McCormick collection.

The small building that held the roaster of Fremont Weir's Blue Bell Barbecue at Plato was destroyed. The barns were wrecked at the farms of William Bolley, Mrs. Laura Wade, and Rolland E. Spearow.

Springfield Township was blessed with an ambitious, hard working woman in the presence of Hilda Hughes. She was born in 1888 on the farm where her great-grandfather, Seth Wallace, had settled in the 1840s. Her grandparents were George W. and Catherine (Griffith) Wallace. Their only child was Hilda's mother,

Students lined up on the steps of the old Brushy Prairie School prior to 1915. Dorothy Harris collection.

Ellen May. She married Sheridan E. Hughes, son of Lewis D. Hughes (who ran a hardware store in LaGrange) and Ellen (Drake) Hughes. Hilda's father was only twenty-four when he was poisoned to death. Martin Hall, a young hired hand at the farm, was charged with murder. This was one of the most sensational trials in LaGrange County history.

Hilda was raised on the farm by her mother and grandmother. (Her widowed mother married Charles C. Cowan twelve years later.) They wanted her to have a good education so she was sent to Northwestern University in Evanston, Illinois, where she earned a bachelor's degree. She was hired to teach at Stroh School and soon became principal of the high school. The following year she became the superintendent of the South Milford schools while also teaching high school classes. In 1920 she was appointed LaGrange County Superintendent of Schools, the first woman to hold that position. She went on to teach at Antioch College and managed the Wallace farm. She is buried in Brushy Chapel Cemetery.

This school was built in 1900 and burned in the winter of 1914. Dorothy Harris collection.

The new Brushy Prairie School was built in 1915 after the previous one burned. It closed in 1964 and is now a private residence. Dorothy Harris collection.

The windmill addition to the general store was added after the store was moved onto U.S. 20. It was a restaurant. Dorothy Harris collection.

Florence Notestine was the teacher of the second and third grades at Brushy Prairie in 1944–1945. She remembers when teachers parked on the hill and sometimes their cars rolled down. During tire rationing, some students put nails in front of the teachers' cars, but the nails were discovered before the tires were ruined. W. B. Sturgis was the principal at Brushy Prairie and Mongo during the 1940s. The students are: (left to right, front row) Carleton Smith, Rolland Smith, Billy Thomas, Robert Myers, Archie Mobley, Donald Myers, Keith Notestine, and Richard Strayer. Second row: Waneta Cosby, Nancy Martin, Nanita Appleman, Shirley Preston, Elaine Weldon (twin), Loraine Weldon (twin), and Virginia Freed. Third row: Norma Talmage, Judy Martin, Bertha McNabb, Marie Mobley, Esther Miller, Charlene McNett, Jeanette Haag, Janet Haag, and Bonnie Ringler. Fourth row: Alan Talmage, Mary Anne Dunbar, Jeanette Troyer, Jeanette Aldrich, Shirley Strayer, Esther Roann Harris, Nancy Jo Ryan, and Janice Garlets. Lloyd W. Goon Photo, Toledo; Dorothy Harris collection.

The old Scott Mill stood on the banks of Pigeon River from 1860 until it was destroyed by fire on February 10, 1968. It was owned by the Boehmer family from 1904 until 1965, first operating as a sawmill and then as a flour mill. It was a power booster station for Northern Indiana Public Service. The Department of Natural Resources owned it. Elster Photo, circa 1914; Blanche Myers collection.

11

Van Buren Township

John and Esther (Smith) Olney (he from Washington County, Ohio, and she from Morgan County, Ohio) heard about cheap government land in Indiana. Traveling in a covered wagon pulled by a yoke of oxen, they came in 1830 to an area near Scott in Van Buren Township. It took them about three weeks to travel the 300 miles. As the story goes, John, son of Sylvanus and Anna (Slack) Olney, stopped his oxen and said, "Here ends my journey," sticking his willow cane, which may have been an ox goad, into the damp earth of the land located six miles west of Howe on the Twin Lakes road. The willow stick took root and grew to a huge tree, twenty-seven and one-half feet in circumference, which shaded the family for generations—111 years, to be exact. The present owner of the farm, Mrs. Leonard (Blanche Olney) Myers, is a member of the fourth generation of the Olney family to live there. Her children, Murlyn, Melvin, Marilyn, and Madeline are the fifth. The farm has passed from John Olney to his son William S., then to grandson Edward Olney, and finally to great-granddaughter Blanche M. Anders. She was adopted at age six by Edward and Anna (Wisler) Olney after their only child had died.

The Olney homestead has the distinction of being a "Century Farm" as designated by the Indiana Historical Society. It has been in the same family for more than 100 years. In this case, it actually has been owned by the Olneys for 164 years! The five original deeds from the government, printed on parchment, are dated 1831, 1832, 1836, signed by President Andrew Jackson, and two dated 1837, signed by President Martin Van Buren.

A small cemetery on the farm contains the graves of Blanche's great-grandparents and two of their children. Some of the other family members are buried at the Sidener Cemetery on State Road 120, back of the Olney farm. William S. Olney was married to Delilah Jane Sidener, daughter of Nicholas and Margaret Sidener. Delilah was a charter member of the first Methodist Episcopal Church in Van Buren Township.

This large group of men and horses appear to be ready to work. Perhaps they are helping a neighbor. Simpson collection.

Right
Inside Hagerty Bros. General Store are Clarence Johnson and Dewey Hagerty. Simpson collection.

Ira Swartzentruber, driving a fancy buckboard about 1917. Born December 12, 1898, to John and Sarah (Weirich) Swartzentruber, he grew up on a farm two miles north of Shipshewana. He married Eva Kline, daughter of James and Katherine, in 1920. Katherine and Gordon were their children. Swartzentruber collection.

Charles Munger), Charles, Harold, and Dewey Hagerty, operated a general store for many years (*Combined Atlases*).

The first doctor was Sidney Cobb, followed by William Fox. Later, Dr. William B. Grubbs and Dr. A. Toms tended to the medical needs of the village. Dr. Grubbs came to Van Buren from Ohio in 1865 when his son, A. G. Grubb (who also became a doctor) was only three. A. G. Grubb moved from Scott to Mongo where he built the hospital which still stands.

Historians have had different views of Scott over the years. In the 1920 *History of Northeast Indiana, Vol. I,* Ira Ford, editor, it is stated that things have changed and "the timber was all cut off and great milling centers robbed this place of its industries forever. No village exists there today." On the other hand, praises were sung regarding the village of Seyberts, a station-point on the Michigan Southern Railroad, located in section 32. It is described as "the only present village within the limits of Van Buren Township" which "consists merely of a station, a few small business houses and plenty of room...with prosperity seen on every hand." Eight years later, G. Earl Crampton, in "History of Van Buren Township," *LaGrange County Centennial,* writes that "Scott is the only village in the township and is a thriving business center." No mention is made of Seyberts.

According to Blanche (Olney) Myers, Bert Fry owned a store at Seyberts' Station during the 1930s. One night someone came to his door. When Fry opened it, he was shot dead and robbed. There was a pickle station at Seyberts, too, says Mrs. Myers. She can remember an old potbellied stove at the store and how the neighborhood men would sit on cream cans and old wooden chairs to play checkers.

Florence Alice, daughter of James and Katherine Kline, married Marion Schrock on November 28, 1918. This picture was taken around that time period. They lived west of Scott. Their children were Maxine and Marion. Swartzentruber collection.

William D. Markley was born in 1868 and lived to be ninety-one. He was a deaf mute who lived with his son and wife, Mr. and Mrs. Sidney Markley, in his later years. He hauled milk to the Howe creamery. Simpson collection.

In the spring of 1907, school children at Scott line up for the photographer. Georgia Haines is the teacher and Nathaniel Davidson is the janitor. Blanche Myers collection.

This red brick school house at Scott was built in 1900. James Kline was a trustee for the two-year high school. Courtesy of Richard Marks.

Scott
Scott
Scott
Scott

Scott School students put on an operetta. Oma Greenwalt was the director. Blanche Myers collection.

Top left
These basketball players have "Scott" monogrammed shirts. Simpson collection.

Bottom left
Scott School children in the first and second grades are shown here in 1943–1944. Blanche Myers collection.

The Scott Mill Park footbridge covered with snow on a winter day. Yoder photo, 1995.

Top right
Scott High School students went to Shipshewana in 1955. Grade school students, along with Clay Township grade school students, were taught at Scott until 1960 when the school closed. The Van Buren Township Community Building is shown as it appears today. Yoder photo, 1995.

Bottom right
The Van Buren Township Merry Maidens 4-H club rides on a float in the Corn School parade in LaGrange. Their theme is, "Cook and sew to catch a beau." Photo circa 1950s. Connelly collection.

VAN BUREN
TWP
AND SEW TO

A modern irrigation system near Howe shows how the landscape has changed in recent years. Many fences have been removed along with trees and vegetation. Yoder photo, 1995.

12

Today

LaGrange County is located on the Indiana-Michigan state line, surrounded by Steuben, Dekalb, Noble, and Elkhart Counties in Indiana and St. Joseph County in Michigan. Largely an agricultural area with some industry, it contains 343 square miles. According to the 1990 Census, the county's population was 29,477 and projected to be 30,306 in 1992.

The main towns, some unincorporated, are LaGrange (the county seat), Howe, Shipshewana, Topeka, Mongo, South Milford, Stroh, and Wolcottville.

The schools, with the exception of nursery schools and day care centers, are: Lakeland School Corporation, Prairie Heights Community Schools, Westview School Corporation, Howe Military School, numerous Amish schools, and the School of Opportunity (for people who are mentally or physically challenged). In Elkhart County is located Bethany Christian High School, a private school established by Mennonites and attended by several LaGrange County students.

According to the *County Profile LaGrange County, Indiana,* written in 1993 by Site Digest and Review, a cooperative economic development program, some of the major employers in the county are: Dometic, Nishikawa Standard, Starcraft RV, Brunswick Marine, Lake Park Industries, Machine Rite Products, Jayco Industries, Mastercraft, Camsco Produce, and Lord's Seeds. A new industry that should be added to the list is Dutch Housing, Inc.

Tourism has increased in recent years; LaGrange County is situated in the middle of northeast Indiana lake country. Many people are attracted to Shipshewana with its auction and huge flea market, antique and craft shops, and good Amish cooking. Pigeon River State Fish and Wildlife Area attracts outdoor people who like to paddle a canoe on the river, fish, hike, and hunt. Wildlife, especially deer and Canada geese, are numerous. Pheasant, dove, and wild turkey hunting are also popular.

Grain mills and lumbering have been important concerns since

Howe Military School was founded in the 1880s and now includes females among its students. It is on State Road 9. Yoder photo, 1995.

Lakeland High School opened in the 1964–1965 school year, across the road from the 4-H fairgrounds. The dome-covered building is the cafeteria. Yoder photo, 1995.

the early days. Farver Lumber Co. is still a vital business in Shipshewana and so is Hubbard Milling Co. (formerly Wolfe Grain, Inc.). Stroh Farm Supply, Inc., Lima Elevator Co., Honeyville Feed Service, Inc., and Hochstedler Grain & Feed Co. at Emma are only a few of the many feed dealers in the county.

Although some of the older establishments are more popular than ever, business and manufacturing in and around the towns has continued to change, both in substance and location. The town of LaGrange has expanded to the north and south. Purity Super Market Inc., Plyley's Candy, and Schlemmer Hardware (which is now a Do-it center) all used to be in the middle of town, but they are now on the southern edge. Gateway Bank is in the same neighborhood. McDonalds has arrived, too. To the north, Shipshewana State Bank has been replaced by Norwest Bank, Pizza Hut is next to Revco (formerly Hook's Drug Store), and CarQuest Auto Parts is across the street on Townline Road instead of in town.

North Pointe Plaza has been developed on the north side of town. It includes the LaGrange County License Branch, Weber's TV & Appliance, and LaGrange Chiropractic, all of which used to be downtown. There is also Dooley's Laundromat, Dunlap Eye Clinic,

Michael Edward Dempsey (February 3, 1969–May 22, 1994), an "All Conference" football player and graduate of Prairie Heights Senior High School, class of 1987, is shown working in April of 1987 on the house being built by his Building Trades class. Dempsey collection.

Prairie Heights Senior High School contains students from both LaGrange and Steuben Counties. It was opened in the fall of 1965 at the intersection of U.S. 20 and the Elmira-Stroh road. Yoder photo, 1995.

The Westview Building Trades class built this house during 1994–1995 on the back side of Emma Lake. Yoder photo, 1995.

Westview Junior-Senior High School is located near Emma in Clay Township. It opened in the 1967–1968 school year. Yoder photo, 1995.

Flexible Personnel, Subway Sandwiches, and Adams Cruise & Travel. Coldwell Banker/Schrock Real Estate and Northside Veterinary Clinic were the first businesses here.

Brown's Drug Store has closed and Norm's Floral Shop has expanded to fill its space. Family Dollar has replaced the W. R. Thomas dime store. A radio station, WTHD (Thunder Country 105.5 FM) is in operation on South High Street. These are only a few of the many changes.

J. O. Mory, Inc., is a prominent heating and air conditioning business in South Milford with branches in surrounding counties. Weiss Trucking Co., Inc., Mongo Country Store, Inc., Pigeon River Trading Post, and Mongo Electronics, Inc., are major forces in Mongo. Yoder Popcorn Co., Inc., is in the Emma area. Topeka has several factories and the Topeka Livestock Draft Horse & Carriage Auction. Yoder's Country Store is an Amish hardware on Hawpatch Road.

Lord's Seeds and Camsco are located in the Brighton area. Many young people are employed every summer by Lord's Seeds to detassel corn. Campbell's Fresh, Inc., (formerly Camsco) is a mushroom farm. Many Hispanics, among others, have been employed there in recent years. As a result, it is not unusual to see signs and notices posted, written in Spanish as well as English. Spanish-speaking educators have also been hired in the local schools.

Stroh and Elmira both have popular fish restaurants: Gropp's Fish of Stroh and Turkey Lake Restaurant and Tavern. Valentine is the home of Lillich Sign Co. Honeyville has a new store to the east on State Road 5 called Tools Unlimited. Patterson's Furniture has closed and the Wolcottville Antique Mall has opened in its place. Bell Gardens, which sells plants and produce, has opened on Woodruff Road.

Venture Welding has started a plant between LaGrange and Howe. Greenfield Research, established east of Howe in the 1980s, makes automotive trim components. There is no longer a hardware in Howe. Purity Super Market has established another grocery next to Society National Bank (formerly State Bank of Lima). The Town Square Restaurant, The Clothes Line (which sells used clothing), Howe Pet Shop, and an ice cream shop have also opened. The Kingsbury House is home to the Better Homes and Gardens/Howe LaGrange Agency.

The Farmers State Bank of Stroh expanded and opened an office in LaGrange on November 7, 1934. It was on the northeast corner of Detroit and Spring Streets in the building previously occupied by The National Bank. The building was remodeled three times. In 1973, the building was sold to the county for a courthouse annex. Farmers State Bank moved into a new building at 220 South Detroit Street. Today, there are six locations to serve the community: Stroh, LaGrange, Topeka, Wolcottville, Shipshewana, and Howe. This year the bank is celebrating eighty years of service.

Creekside School, one of many Amish schools in the county, opened in 1985–1986 on land formerly owned by William Schrock. It is a little east of 100E and 250N. Yoder photo, 1995.

Menno-Hof was built during 1986–1988 to give visitors an idea about the Mennonite and Amish basis for existence. It opened May 2, 1988. Harvey Chupp, Steve Dintaman, and director Tim Lichti, among many others, helped plan the programs and helped build the barn and house. It is located on State Road 5 in Shipshewana. Former President Jimmy Carter and his wife paid a visit in May of this year. Yoder photo, 1995.

Brown's Drug Store has been "serving the community since 1896," but in spring 1995, it closed its doors. The community will miss it. Yoder photo, 1995.

Campbell's Fresh, Inc., grows mushrooms for Campbell's soup. It is located near Brighton. Yoder photo, 1995.

Glenda Myers-Todd and her husband, Greg Todd, saw a print entitled "Yesteryear," which inspired them to have this spacious Victorian home built in 1994. Ervin Miller of LaGrange was the builder. The floor plan was designed by Greg and Glenda. It was totally decorated by Glenda Myers-Todd with all white walls and woodwork and beige carpet. The furnishings are a mix of antique and contemporary. The woodwork includes plinth blocks and rosettes with fluted jambs. The tower is fifty-two feet high from the top of the cupola to ground level. It has an 8' x 8' tower room. An open oak stairway leads to an 18' x 20' landing area which has a stairway accessible to the tower. There are two gas log fireplaces and several rooms of ceramic tile floors. It has a full basement and an eight-sided turret. The Todds refer to their ten-acre estate as "Yesteryear." Yoder photo, 1995.

This is a view behind the teller's box at Farmers State Bank years ago at the Detroit and Spring Streets location. Courtesy of Miles S. Perkins.

Farmers State Bank built this new bank building next door to the post office and moved into it in 1973. Miles S. Perkins has been the president since the beginning of 1976. Yoder photo, 1995.

The Bir Hotel became the Day Hotel. Later it was home to the Moose Lodge. Now it has been completely renovated to house the LaGrange County Council on Aging. Yoder photo, 1995.

Plato Methodist Church and cemetery were established in the 1800s. They are located half a mile south of Plato. The eariliest burials were in the 1830s. D. Crandle, W. Maxwell, and L. E. Deal were commissioners at the time the Methodist Church's cornerstone was laid in 1886. Yoder photo, 1995.

Plato Mennonite Church was established on U.S. 20 just east of where the old store used to be. Yoder photo, 1995.

Amish horses and buggies beside the hitching rail behind the LaGrange County Courthouse on a snowy day. Yoder photo, 1995.

Following page
Nasby Dam is a V-shaped dam on the Pigeon River between Mongo and Ontario. It is a popular fishing spot and a good place to launch a canoe. Yoder photo, 1995.

The old St. Joseph Valley Line Depot on North Detroit Street was built to accommodate the railroad's customers (1905–1918). When the railroad closed, it became a home and later an antique shop. It is now home to the LaGrange County Chamber of Commerce. Yoder photo, 1995.

An Amish man is using three horses to work the field in the spring. It is quite a contrast to the modern machinery used by some farmers in the county. Yoder photo, 1995.

Following page
April 30, 1995, was a rainy day on Detroit Street in LaGrange. Yoder photo.

FSB
FARMERS
STATE
BANK
Radio
Shack

H&R BLOCK
INCOME TAX
PEPSI
EAGLES 3325
FOE

This is a copy of the mural entitled *Corn School.* It was placed at the north end of the lobby above the LaGrange postmaster's office door in 1941. According to the *LaGrange Standard,* it is oil on canvas, 10' 10" wide by 5' 7" high. Jessie Hull Mayer painted it under the auspices of the Fine Arts of the Public Buildings Administration, Federal Works Agency. She graduated from the Yale School of Fine Arts. The mural depicts the livestock parade at the county fair held in LaGrange. The red brick courthouse is in the background. Mural by Jessie Hull Mayer, 1941; LaGrange Post Office; Yoder photo; courtesy of Postmaster John Cochard.

Bibliography

Books

Borntreger, Hans. *A History of the First Settlers of the Amish Mennonites and the Establishment of Their First Congregation in the State of Indiana, Along With a Short Account of the Division Which Took Place in This Church.* Elkhart, Indiana: Mennonite Publishing Company, 1907; Kalona, Iowa: Enos H. Miller, 1961; Middlebury, Indiana: Pleasant Ridge Printers, 1986; Sugarcreek, Ohio: Schlabach Printers (First printing in English by Dan A. Hochstetler), 1988.

Current, Robert and Leonore Current, comp. *Cemeteries of LaGrange County Indiana, 1832–1982.* Dallas, Texas: Taylor Publishing Company, 1984.

Ford, Ira, editor, et al. *History of Northeast Indiana: LaGrange, Steuben, Noble, and Dekalb Counties, Volume I.* Chicago and New York: The Lewis Publishing Company, 1920.

Hanan, John W., comp. *LaGrange County Centennial History, 1828–1928.* LaGrange, Indiana: LaGrange Publishing Company, 1928.

Kilver, M. D., editor. *A History of Lima Township LaGrange County, Indiana.* Howe, Indiana: Bicentennial Committee of the Howe, Indiana Lions Club, 1976.

Kintner, Elgin P. *Edward Kintner and Glada Snyder Ancestral Genealogy and Tour Guide.* Maryville, Tennessee: Elgin P. Kintner, M.D., 1994.

LaGrange County Historical Society, comp. *Combined 1874 & 1893 Illustrated Historical Atlas of LaGrange County Indiana: With New Indexes & Additional Contents. 1874 Atlas.* Chicago: Andreas and Baskin; *1893 Atlas.* LaGrange, Indiana: LaGrange Standard Printing Company. Reprint (2 vols. in 1), Knightstown, Indiana: The Bookmark, 1975.

LaGrange Sesquicentennial Book Committee. *My Town, Your Town—LaGrange—1836–1986.* Edited by Sandy Yoder. Dallas, Texas: Taylor Publishing Company, 1986.

Myers, Blanche M. (Olney). *Illustrated History of Van Buren (Scott) Village Indiana.* Middlebury Graphic Arts: Middlebury, Indiana, 1982.

Report of the Adjutant General of the State of Indiana, Volume VI. Indianapolis: Samuel M. Douglass, State Printer, 1866.

[Rerick, John H., et al.]. *Counties of LaGrange and Noble, Indiana: Historical and Biographical.* Chicago: F. A. Battey and Company, 1882.

Topeka Area Historical Society. *Celebrating a Century, 1893–1993.* Edited by Maggie Glick. Nappanee, Indiana: Evangel Press, 1993.

Wolf, Julie, editor. *A Patchwork Sampler: Collective Stories of a Community.* Shipshewana, Indiana: Shipshewana Centennial Jubilee Committee, 1989.

Articles and Pamphlets

Case, Riley L. "History of Woodruff." 18 June 1984.

"County Profile LaGrange County, Indiana," *Site Digest and Review.* Indianapolis: Wabash Valley Power Association, Inc., July 1993.

Forst, Marguerite. "The birth of Elmira," *LaGrange Standard,* 13 March 1969.

____. "Stroh—the village which cement built," *LaGrange Standard,* 25 June 1975.

McKibben, J. Scott. "Valentine." 14 February 1952.

Reed, Bert M. "History of Stroh," *LaGrange Standard,* 23 January 1969.

Newspapers

LaGrange Standard
The Stroh Times

Index

About the Photographer

Robert Yoder

Robert Yoder, the author's husband, is an amateur photographer who became interested in photography while taking pictures of Civil War tombstones. He shot the recent photographs and rephotographed the historic ones. He relies on professionals for developing.

A LaGrange native, Robert graduated from Indiana University, Fort Wayne campus, with a degree in geology. Most of his life, however, he has worked as an industrial electrician.

Robert Yoder, photographer; Sandy Yoder photo.

About the Author

Sandra Connelly Yoder

Sandy Yoder, author; Lifetouch National School Studios photo.

Sandra (Sandy) Connelly Yoder was born in St. Joseph County, Michigan, but has always lived in Indiana. She graduated from LaGrange High School. She has a B.A. and M.S. from Indiana University, Fort Wayne campus.

Past positions held are: English teacher in Allen and LaGrange Counties, special education teacher, media center coordinator, director of Job Training Partnership Act in LaGrange and Kosciusko Counties, reading consultant, private school teacher, English instructor at Davenport College, and guidance counselor at Prairie Heights Middle School.

Presently, she is part-time guidance counselor at Prairie Heights High School and a sponsor of the Indiana Future Educators in Action. She is on the board of directors for the LaGrange County Historical Society Inc., and also belongs to the Indiana Historical Society. The LaGrange Sesquicentennial Book Committee published *My Town, Your Town—LaGrange—1836–1986* which Sandy edited. She has one son, three grandsons, and one granddaughter. Her interests are collecting antiques and writing. She and her husband like to travel and to research genealogy and LaGrange's participation in the Civil War.

LHS
GRAN
GRAN